that dition certain devices, moods, and ideas that permeate his total work.

Consideration of Shelley's app'' tion of the Gothic mode as ~ for psychological analv~' by a brief introdv~ teristics of the G erature. Chapter 1 ley's two Gothic no ..nes of youthful poetry, an .. Mab as they relate to the Gothic mode.

Alastor, one of Shelley's first major poems, receives lengthy exposition in chapter 2 to demonstrate how the protagonist's conflict between the real and the ideal can be understood best in terms of Gothic conventions. Chapter 3 begins by elaborating on Gothic features established earlier and moves on to examine a number of Shelley's major poems for their Gothic content, how this content affects the poems' meaning, and finally the process by which Gothic elements are refined or eventually disappear in such works as "Mont Blanc," "Ode to the West Wind," and *Prometheus Unbound.*

In chapter 4, analysis is devoted solely to *The Cenci* and its Gothic elements, so that the disastrous implications of the Gothic sensibility are revealed. The conclusion postulates that the Gothic tradition offered Shelley a significant medium through which to approach the dark as well as the light side of man's experience.

The Dark Angel

The Dark Angel

Gothic Elements In Shelley's Works

John V. Murphy

Lewisburg
Bucknell University Press

London: Associated University Presses

© 1975 by Associated University Presses, Inc.

Associated University Presses, Inc.
Cranbury, New Jersey 08512

Associated University Presses
108 New Bond Street
London W1Y OQX, England

Library of Congress Cataloging in Publication Data

Murphy, John V
    The dark angel.

    Bibliography: p.
    1. Shelley, Percy Bysshe, 1792-1822—Criticism and in-
terpretation. I. Title.
PR5438.M8   821'.7   73-8304
ISBN 0-8387-1407-2

Printed in the United States of America

For
Austin Warren
and
Richard Morfit

Contents

Preface

Shelley's two early novels *Zastrozzi* and *St. Irvyne* are, as
many scholars have noted, obviously connected to the tradi-
tion of the Gothic novel; as well, two volumes of early poetry
contain Gothic elements and his tragedy *The Cenci* has been
associated with the Gothic drama. Scholarship has failed to
note adequately, however, that Gothic elements also play a
major role in much of his mature poetry, where they assume
a particular importance. The purpose of this study is to
indicate those elements and to define their significance in
relation to typical Shelleyan themes.

After a survey of Shelley's early Gothic work, certain
conventions such as the hero-villain figure, the quest-curse
motif, dream-vision experience, and "atmospheric" imag-
ery are emphasized when they appear in his later poetry.
Furthermore, terror, horror, anguish, guilt, and melancholy
will be noted when it can be established that they are particu-
larly helpful in gaining an accurate understanding of the
poems. All of these characteristics provide a means of dem-
onstrating that Shelley takes from the Gothic tradition cer-
tain devices, moods, and ideas that permeate his total work.
Although much of the obvious Gothic trapping is lost, it
becomes apparent that the major poetry uses Gothic traits
for very serious ends. This last consideration must be
clarified: I do not claim that Shelley's mature poetry is
Gothic; rather, my contention is that Gothic elements work

in many of the major poems to enhance the poet's intention. Whether in crude or refined form, the Gothic tradition repeatedly furnishes Shelley with a framework to express his sensibility.

Analysis will indicate that Gothic elements employed in the early works to instill terror, fear, and other strong emotions, primarily for their own sake, have, in the mature works, become important psychic instruments of quite another kind: Shelley uses the resources of the Gothic tradition to engender an awareness of complex and ambiguous mental attitudes and exploits Gothic conventions for acute psychological analysis that, moreover, usually serves a didactic intention of personal or philosophical import.

The study of Shelley's application of the Gothic mode as an agency for psychological analysis is preceded by a brief introduction to the characteristics of the Gothic sensibility in literature. Chapter 1 then examines Shelley's two Gothic novels, two volumes of early poetry, and *Queen Mab* as they relate to the Gothic mode. *Alastor*, one of Shelley's first major poems, receives lengthy exposition in chapter 2 to demonstrate how the protagonist's conflict between the real and the ideal can be understood best in terms of Gothic conventions. Chapter 3 begins by elaborating on Gothic features established earlier and then moves on to examine succinctly a number of Shelley's major poems for their Gothic content, how this content affects the poems' meaning, and finally the process by which Gothic elements are refined or eventually disappear in such works as "Mont Blanc," "Ode to the West Wind," and *Prometheus Unbound*. In chapter 4, analysis is devoted solely to *The Cenci* and its Gothic elements so that the disastrous implications of the Gothic sensibility are revealed. The conclusion postulates that the Gothic tradition offered Shelley a significant medium through which to approach the dark as well as the light side of man's experience.

Acknowledgments

The lengthy and involved undertaking that is necessarily a part of a scholarly adventure enlists the energies and talents of many people besides the writer. Proper appreciation for the valuable assistance others gave to this study would be difficult to express here. I would, however, like to welcome into these pages certain colleagues, friends, and relatives who read, listened, questioned, argued, and advised me on matters central to the writing of the book.

In this regard, Professor Earl J. Schulze, under whose stimulating guidance and encouragement the original argument developed, warrants deep thanks for his fine criticisms, scholarly advice, and warm friendship. Professors William Coles, Robert Stilwell, John Mersereau, Harry Garvin, and Michael Payne also aided me greatly in refining both the style and thought of the text.

Indebtedness of quite another kind, a kind difficult to place solely in relation to a particular scholarly endeavor, I will always owe to Professor Austin Warren and the late Professor Richard Morfit. Over the past years, these dear friends and fine mentors have, both gently and rigorously, counseled my academic direction and been the most sustaining influence on it.

Finally, I wish to thank those who read much of the material and, indirectly, helped shape many of the ideas that make up this study of Shelley. In particular, I deeply appreciate the assistance of Professors Ralph Berets, Robert Levy, James S. Torrens, S.J., and Mr. David Wrubel. Perhaps they would not profess a great liking for Shelley, but at least they aided me in formulating more clearly my own reasons for enjoying him. To my wife, for her patience, sacrifice, and help, I acknowledge an inestimable debt of thanks.

Introduction

Shelleyans have long been irritated by Matthew Arnold's damning conclusion to his essay on the poet of *Prometheus Unbound*: "The man Shelley, in very truth, is not entirely sane, and Shelley's poetry is not entirely sane either. The Shelley of actual life is a vision of beauty and radiance, indeed, but availing nothing, effecting nothing. And in poetry, no less than in life, he is 'a beautiful and ineffectual angel, beating in the void his luminous wings in vain.' "[1] When one aligns Arnold's assertion with the obvious energetic revolutionary activity that courses through Shelley's young manhood, there is little doubt that either Arnold is misguided or modern biographers and critics are. For example, both N. I. White and K. N. Cameron[2] insist that Shelley's "luminous wings" beat violently to fan the revolutionary fires of the early 1800s'. Arnold's cavalier dismissal of Shelley as an "ineffectual angel" suggests that the shortcoming is not in Shelley's perception of his times or of himself, but, instead, in the capacity of Arnold to understand what the angel was trying to do. Rather than a spirit of "sweetness and light," I would suggest that Shelley relies on

---

[1] Matthew Arnold, "Shelley," in *Poetry and Criticism of Matthew Arnold*, ed. A. Dwight Culler (Boston, 1961), p. 380.

[2] Newman Ivey White, *Shelley*, 2 vols. (New York, 1940); Kenneth Neil Cameron, *The Young Shelley* (New York, 1962).

the presence of a bitter and dark angel to illuminate his greatest visions.

One can begin at a particular point in time to introduce the side of Shelley's nature that is not all beautiful or radiant — a somber, serious nature that rises to the light only by understanding the darkness about it. From his exuberant childhood energies, we begin to distinguish how an intense and lively imagination started playing with occult interests that would eventually lead to very threatening demonic visions:

> As a leader and entertainer of his younger sisters Bysshe fancied himself tremendously. He told them tales of the legendary Great Tortoise that haunted Warnham Pond, where the family sometimes went for a picnic dinner; and of the Old Snake that led a peaceful existence for many years in the Field Place grounds until accidentally slain by a gardener. . . . He tapped the ceiling with a stick to discover to them a secret passage which must certainly be beyond; he drew graphic pictures of an old gray alchemist who dwelt in a garret that was closed against their explorations. . . . Fantastic costumes were devised in which to personate spirits or fiends while Bysshe, as the archfiend, rushed through a passage with a flaming liquid in a portable stove.[3]

These tales and pranks are only a small part of the history of the spirited young poet; and his years at Syon House Academy, Eton College, and the brief stay at Oxford are, in many ways, extensions of his amusements at home: he became engrossed in chemistry, electricity, magnetism, occult sciences, and, as one might expect from his particular bent of mind, the Gothic novel. Often termed "Blue Books" or "Shilling Shockers,"these puerile novels carry such titles as *Don Algonah, or the Sorceress of Montillo; The Black Forest, or The Cavern of Horrors; The Subterraneous Passage, or Gothic Cell;* and *The Cavern of Horrors, or Miseries*

---

[3]White, 1:25.

of Miranda, a Neapolitan Tale. Of much more importance
for Shelley's developing interest in the Gothic mode, how-
ever, was his exposure to such noted authors as Horace
Walpole, Ann Radcliffe, M. G. Lewis, William Godwin,
Charlotte Dacre, and Charles Brockden Brown. By the end
of the eighteenth century, these writers had firmly estab-
lished the Gothic tradition, and Shelley freely borrowed
their conventions for the novels and poetry he wrote be-
tween the ages of sixteen and eighteen.[4]

At this point, particular comments and definitions that are
relevant to an understanding of the Gothic tradition and its
special sensibility must be provided. For my purposes, a
survey of Gothic conventions and the various functions they
classically perform is best taken from the writings of such
avid students of the Gothic as Horace Walpole, Montague
Summers, Eino Railo, Bertrand Evans, Mario Praz, Eleanor
Sickels, and Devendra P. Varma.[5] These authors focus our
attention on both the external and the internal characteris-
tics of the Gothic tradition so that insights for the total study
are introduced. Since Gothic features have already been
carefully analyzed by others, the review that follows is
largely linear and discursive. The finer application of this
discussion will appear when the operation of the Gothic is
related directly to Shelley's works.

In the preface to the first edition of *The Castle of Otranto*,
Horace Walpole offers an idea that is crucial when distin-
guishing effects produced by the Gothic: ''Terror, the
author's principal engine, prevents the story from ever lan-
guishing; and it is so often contrasted by pity that the mind is

---

[4]See Edith Birkhead, *The Tale of Terror* (London, 1921), pp. 122-26 and A. M. D.
Hughes, *The Nascent Mind of Shelley* (Oxford, 1947), pp. 29-38 for reference to the
exact sources of Shelley's borrowings.
[5]Sir Kenneth Clark's *The Gothic Revival*, Paul Frankl's *The Gothic*, A. O.
Lovejoy's ''The First Gothic Revival and the Return to Nature,'' and John
Ruskin's *The Stones of Venice* aid one significantly in understanding the Gothic
sensibility, but since their primary interest is in architecture, my definitions will be
restricted to those who have studied the Gothic from a literary point of view.

kept up in a constant vicissitude of interesting passions.''[6] Montague Summers's *The Gothic Quest* adds to Walpole's observation by stating that ''aspiration, yearning desire, mystery, wonder, certainly approaches near the heart of the matter, and we shall find that from those essential elements spring the characteristics of the Gothic novel.''[7] A more helpful and particular discussion of terror and mystery is found in Eino Railo's *The Haunted Castle:*

> We can regard suspense as the preliminary and preparatory stage of terror; this in itself is a cumulative and continuous state of mind that becomes transformed, when a certain stage of intensification is reached, into a state of petrified terror, a paralysis that also manifests itself physically. Withdrawal from it is only possible by a change of conditions caused by physical movement, in which moreover the outward contact with the cause of terror is broken. One notices accordingly that the means used by terror-writers to lead the reader by degrees to an ultimate state of terror are the creation of suspense, and its subsequent maintenance and intensification.[8]

An example from Ann Radcliffe's *The Mysteries of Udolpho* illustrates Railo's point and provides us with certain attributes that are central to the Gothic mode. The following scene occurs while Emily and Dorothée are exploring the chamber where the Marchioness died, and they notice that the pall on the bed seems to move:

> Emily attempted to go, but Dorothée stood fixed and gazing upon the bed; and, at length, said — ''It is only the wind, that waves it, ma'amselle; we have left all the doors open: see how the air waves the lamp, too. — It is only the wind.''
> She had scarcely uttered these words, when the pall was more violently agitated than before; but Emily, somewhat ashamed of her terrors, stepped back to the bed, willing to be convinced that

[6]Horace Walpole, *The Castle of Otranto* (New York, 1963), p. 16.
[7]Montague Summers, *The Gothic Quest* (London, 1938), p. 24.
[8]Eino Railo, *The Haunted Castle* (New York, 1964), p. 319.

the wind only had occasioned her alarm; when, as she gazed within the curtains, the pall moved again, and in the next moment, the apparition of a human countenance rose above it.[9]

Radcliffe's method is to develop precisely the external Gothic situation; that is, the influence of nature on human passions, the forbidding aura surrounding the castle of Udolpho itself, the gloomy and mysterious chambers within, and strange, sinister figures and villains. Then, through a lengthy process of building suspense, she increases the tension in a particular scene so that terror is certain. As we see in the quoted passage, her techniques of suggestion allow the mind to move back and forth between natural (the wind) and supposedly supernatural (the apparition) agencies. Such adroit manipulation of her materials ensures the atmosphere of suspense, mystery, and terror that Radcliffe deemed necessary for her purposes.

Railo describes further certain features that are externally common to the Gothic tradition. For example, the use of moonlight, shadows, trees, rustling leaves, storms, and other sensually perceivable phenomena are important to support larger issues such as the Gothic hero-villan, the persecuted heroine, the conniving monk, the mysterious figure of the Wandering Jew, ghosts, demonic beings, and the disturbed mind. In alliance with Railo's study of the Gothic novel, Bertrand Evans finds that Gothic drama offers a long list of stage properties that resemble those in the novel: "the atmosphere of mystery, the spiral staircase . . . the secret panel . . . the haunted chamber, the subterranean passage . . . the convent . . . the fluttering candle flame . . . the gloomy tyrant."[10] Though we consider them outward manifestations of the Gothic, these elements are critical because they draw our attention to the mood and situation that often determine the Gothic pattern we seek.

[9]Ann Radcliffe, *The Mysteries of Udolpho* (London, 1966), pp. 535-36.
[10]Bertrand Evans, *Gothic Drama from Walpole to Shelley* (Berkeley, 1947), p. 1.

On another level, Mario Praz's *The Romantic Agony* imposes an acute psychological and comparative basis for an understanding of the horrid, the grotesque, the morbid, the erotic, and the satanic that regularly appear in Gothic literature. One of the most important characteristics of this literature, says Praz, is that "the discovery of Horror as a source of delight and beauty ended by reacting on men's actual conception of beauty itself: The Horrid, from being a category of the Beautiful, ended by becoming one of its essential elements, and the 'beautifully horrid' passed by insensible degrees into the 'horribly beautiful'."[11] This particular point is brought out perfectly by M. G. Lewis.

The Monk makes use of murder, rape, incest, matricide, black magic, and satanic forces to accomplish its ends. Lewis imploys all the familiar conventions of the Gothic, but he usually depends heavily on sensationalism and grotesque situations to horrify his reader. One instance of such practice occurs when Ambrosio, the monk, tries to rape Antonia; his plans, however, are momentarily foiled by Elvira, the girl's mother. With all too vivid detail, Lewis describes how Ambrosio smothers Elvira with a pillow:

> The monk continued to kneel upon her breast, witnessed without mercy the convulsive trembling of her limbs beneath him, and sustained with inhuman firmness the spectacle of her agonies, when soul and body were on the point of separating. Those agonies at length were over. She ceased to struggle for life. The monk took off the pillow, and gazed upon her. Her face was covered with a frightful blackness: her limbs moved no more: the blood was chilled in her veins: her heart had forgotten to beat; and her hands were stiff and frozen. Ambrosio beheld before him that once noble and majestic form, now become a corse, cold, senseless, and disgusting.[12]

Only after Ambrosio has raped and murdered Antonia does

---

[11]Mario Praz, *The Romantic Agony* (London, 1933), p. 27.
[12]M. G. Lewis, *The Monk* (New York, 1952), p. 297.

he discover that she is his sister and Elvira his mother. But this turn of events compares mildly to many others in the novel, and the brutal tale that Lewis writes accentuates certain important elements for later Gothic authors, including Shelley. The turn toward the "horribly beautiful" insisted on going beyond terror and employed satanic figures, blasphemy, rape, incest, murder, and excessive cruelty to penetrate deeper into the dark side of human experience, actual or imagined.

One can argue that the exploration of terror and horror has, ultimately, a larger focus behind it than mere sensationalism. Eleanor Sickels enlarges our understanding of the dimension that the Gothic sensibility can assume by relating it to attitudes and interests that develop out of a religious consciousness:

> the elements which terror-romanticism took from the medieval revival were the very elements which it had in common with black religious melancholy. It took the backgrounds of dim cathedrals, midnight churchyards, ghastly charnel houses, and gloomy monastic ruins. It took the death theme, and embroidered it with all the terrors of physical corruption and spectral visitation. It took the theme of sin, and added domestic and exotic demonology, age-old tales of contracts with Satan, and the expiatory sufferings of the Wandering Jew. And out of the theme of sin, which is never far from the theme of death, it built its arch-types — the criminal monk, the tyrant, the strong dark hero inwardly consumed by remorse.[13]

Sickels directs our attention repeatedly to the possibility that the Gothic tradition, because it emphasizes the constant conflict between good and evil — with evil usually winning out — is a way of facing both physical and metaphysical questions of evil that relate this world to a spiritual one.

Finally, D. P. Varma's *The Gothic Flame* goes so far as to raise the Gothic tradition to the level of mysticism. First his

---

[13]Eleanor Sickels, *The Gloomy Egoist* (New York, 1932), pp. 159-60.

study reviews the major ideas common to the authors already mentioned (that is, an interest in the past, in suspense, guilt, anguish, melancholy, the grotesque, terror, horror, etc.) , but he then pursues his argument beyond any of the former discussions by insisting that the primary concern of the Gothic sensibility is spiritual or metaphysical:

> The Gothic attitude relates the individual with the infinite Universe, as do great religions and mystic philosophy. Such a mind grasps the infinite and the finite, the abstract and the concrete, the whole and the nothingness as one: and from the tension between the human and the divine is kindled the votive glow that ever contemplates the world of Gothic mystery.[14]

Because it claims too much, Varma's idea is misleading and mostly beside the point for a study of Shelly's relationship to the Gothic mode. Only in one respect does Varma really help us: "the tension between the human and the divine," the real and the ideal, that appears in so much of Shelley's mature poetry and in *The Cenci* is distinctly part of his Gothic background, but whereas Varma understands his topic from a mystical point of view, my argument asserts that Shelley holds to a symbolic and psychological level that employs the Gothic solely for human ends.

What I have tried to introduce, or recall, so far is the fact that there are definite conventions that constitute the Gothic mode and these features serve a definite purpose, for it is the combination of certain elements and a particular method of presenting them that determine the Gothic sensibility. A historical survey of the Gothic tradition in England could certainly include the work of James Thomson in *The Seasons*; the "graveyard school" of poetry written by Parnell, Young, Blair, Collins, and the Wartons; the odes and

---

[14]Devendra P. Varma, *The Gothic Flame* (London, 1957), pp. 15-16. For excellent bibliographies of countless articles, essays, and books on the Gothic tradition, see Varma, pp. 245-59 and Montague Summers, *A Gothic Bibliography* (New York, 1964).

"The Bard" of Thomas Gray; Macpherson's *Ossian*; Bishop Percy's *Reliques of Ancient English Poetry*; and certain works of all the great Romantic poets. As well, the prose fiction of Richardson and Smollett contains some Gothic elements that are later fully developed by Walpole, Radcliffe, Lewis, Godwin, Dacre, and Maturin. The array of characters, settings, moods, motifs, and themes that these authors produce established the Gothic tradition, and examination will demonstrate how Shelley is distinctly a part of that tradition by noting the conventions he employs.

Further examples from Gothic writers or from students of the Gothic would be essentially tedious and fruitless at this point. My discussion is designed simply to remind the reader of specific external characteristics of the Gothic (ghosts, castles, villains, heroines, crime, graveyards, etc.) and common internal preoccupations (the conflict between reason and imagination, "the dark sublime," the mysterious and inexplicable in human life, the savage and terrible, gloom and melancholy, and the struggle between the flesh and the spirit) that are important in distinguishing a major area of Shelley's sensibility. The most appropriate place to begin an analysis of this sensibility is in his two early novels, for, as one scholar has stated:

> In the novel it was the function of Gothic to open horizons beyond social patterns, rational decisions, and institutionally approved emotions; in a word, to enlarge the sense of reality and its impact on the human being. It became then a great liberator of feeling. It acknowledged the nonrational — in the world of things and events, occasionally in the realm of the transcendental, ultimately and most persistently in the depths of the human being.[15]

Progression from the early novels to the early poetry, the mature poetry, and *The Cenci* will provide the evidence

---

[15] Robert B. Heilman, "Charlotte Brontë's 'New' Gothic," in *Victorian Literature*, ed. Austin Wright (New York, 1961), p. 84.

needed to support the thesis that the Gothic tradition was central to Shelley's explorations into "the depths of the human being."

The Dark Angel

'For know there are two worlds of life and death:
One that which thou beholdest; but the other
Is underneath the grave, where do inhabit
The shadows of all forms that think and live
Till death unite them and they part no more;
Dreams and the light imaginings of men,
And all that faith creates or love desires,
Terrible, strange, sublime and beauteous shapes.'

—*Prometheus Unbound*

Sorrow, terror, anguish, despair itself, are often the chosen expressions of an approximation to the highest good. Our sympathy in tragic fiction depends on this principle; tragedy delights by affording a shadow of the pleasure which exists in pain.

—"A Defence of Poetry"

1
Shelley's Juvenilia

Because the critical progression this chapter seeks to emphasize moves from external to internal Gothic features, Shelley's two novels, *Zastrozzi* and *St. Irvyne; or, the Rosicrucian*, and his two volumes of early poetry, *Original Poetry by Victor and Cazire* and *Posthumous Fragments of Margaret Nicholson*, will illustrate the presence and function of particular Gothic conventions that were used before he wrote his long revolutionary poem *Queen Mab*.[1] Except for this last-mentioned poem, which will serve as a transition between the early and the mature work, all four volumes of Shelley's juvenilia were written and published within the space of a year and a half; thus, one should not anticipate significant change in the young author's techniques or thematic interests until *Queen Mab* appears. Nonetheless, the process of discovering why the Gothic tradition is important in studying Shelley requires a somewhat full description of certain elements that will be analyzed later, in the mature poetry.

Since other students of Shelley have already adequately

---

[1]Though there is obvious indication that Gothic conventions are at work in Shelley's "The Assassins" (1814) and "The Coliseum" (1817), they have not been included in this discussion because of their fragmentary nature.

covered many aspects of his juvenilia,[2] my study will center
on such topics as the hero-villain idea, the distempered
mind, the dream-vision technique, and characteristic Gothic
imagery and trappings. After the germination of these ele-
ments has been described and defined, their persistence and
refinement will be better understood and appreciated as we
proceed. But perhaps a cautionary note and Shelley's own
spoofing with the Gothic mode should be indicated here so
that a balanced perspective is maintained.

Cameron points out that one must hesitate before taking
Shelley's two novels very seriously:

> That Shelley, as a youngster, was genuinely interested in the
> mysterious and the occult, we have ample evidence, and in his
> novels he was, from time to time, carried away by his subject —
> especially by the character of Ginotti in *St. Irvyne*—but he
> wrote largely with his tongue in his cheek—delighting, at times,
> in parodying his own style—aware, as he was writing the
> novels, of their inherent ridiculousness, but interested in a
> quick, schoolboy fame.[3]

And a letter that Shelley wrote to a friend, inviting him for a
visit, supports Cameron's observation:

> The avenue is composed of vegetable substances moulded in
> the form of trees called by the multitude Elm trees. . . . they all
> lean as if the wind had given them a box on the ear, you
> therefore will know them—Stalk along the road towards
> them—and mind and keep yourself concealed as my Mother
> brings a bloodstained stiletto which she purposes to make you
> bathe in the life-blood of her enemy.
> Never mind the Death-demons, and skeletons dripping with
> the putrefaction of the grave, that occasionally may blast your
> straining eyeball.—Persevere even though Hell and destruction
> should yawn beneath your feet.

[2]See particularly J. C. Jeaffreson, *The Real Shelley*, vol. 1 (London, 1885); A. M.
D. Hughes, *The Nascent Mind of Shelley*; (Oxford, 1947); D. G. Halliburton,
"Shelley's 'Gothic' Novels," *K-SJ* 16 (1967): 39-49; and Eleanor Sickels, "Shelley
and Charles Brockden Brown," *PMLA* 45 (1930); 1116-28.

[3]Kenneth Neil Cameron, *The Young Shelley* (New York, 1962), p. 43.

Think of all this at the frightful hour of midnight, when the Hell-demon leans over your sleeping form and inspires those thoughts which eventually will lead you to the gates of destruction.[4]

One should not, however, readily conclude from the above quotations that Shelley's extravagant stories and poetry carry no lasting import, for in his juvenilia are found themes and conventions that faithfully recur later: the persecuted and defiant protagonist, revenge, the bond between good and evil, conflicting and ambiguous circumstances, the supernatural, and antipathy toward religion, oppressive government, and social institutions.

Cameron and most other scholars have too completely disassociated the young from the mature Shelley. They prefer to see *Queen Mab* (1813) as his first significant work and incline to neglect a positive relationship between Shelley's early and late periods. Though there is some justification for this view, it is, finally, too restrictive and disregards a major means of understanding Shelley more completely than we do at present. Fortunately, a few students of Shelley have suggested, though they have not pursued, the relationship we seek. For example, F. L. Jones, in a brief article, supports my thesis when he concludes that "in the very midst of his boyish romancing we find Shelley treating ideas and situations which are fundamental in his own character and which are directly related to *Alastor, Epipsychidion* and 'The Witch of Atlas'."[5] Jones notes that Shelley's early novels are indeed important gauges against which we can measure not so much a development and change in the poet's thought and artistic practice as a refinement and precision in his

---

[4]*The Complete Works of Percy Bysshe Shelley*, ed. Roger Ingpen and Walter E. Peck, 10 vols. (New York, 1965), 8: 9-10.

[5]F. L. Jones, "*Alastor* Foreshadowed in *St. Irvyne*," *PMLA* 49 (1934): 971. Along this same line, see also Newman Ivey White, *Shelley* (New York, 1940), 1: 90; Eino Railo, *The Haunted Castle* (New York, 1964), p. 155; and Floyd H. Stovall, *Desire and Restraint in Shelley* (Durham, N. C., 1931), p. 12.

thinking. A review of those novels and their Gothic features
will initiate a coherent pattern for a total investigation.

I

In Shelley's first published prose work, *Zastrozzi* (1810), the
reader immediately recognizes the major conventional
characters of Gothic fiction: in Zastrozzi the mysterious,
dark hero-villain, in Verezzi the distraught and highly sensi-
tive victim, in Matilda the violent and seductive "fatal
woman," and in Julia the innocent but implicated bystander.
As well, there are tyrannical figures of church and state and
external scenery that includes castles, mountains, woods,
and storms. Finally, the usual interest in murder, revenge,
guilt, anguish, terror, and, in general, defiance of human and
divine laws is also present. Shortly it will be necessary to
discuss the psychological relationship that exists between
these particular types of characters, settings, and themes or
motifs, but for the moment let us assume that Shelley's
obvious intention is merely to terrify and thrill his audience,
while, simultaneously, touching on such dangerous and un-
orthodox topics as free love, social and religious tyranny,
and atheism.

    In the role of hero-villain, Zastrozzi plays a double func-
tion that conforms to the Gothic pattern of creating mixed
and ambiguous reactions in the mind of the reader: on the
one hand, we must condemn the villain's evil acts and the
tragedy they produce, while, on the other hand, we come to
sympathize with his motives and approve of his courage.
Since the novel's major theme is revenge, the code that
Zastrozzi follows is very like the one found in Elizabethan
and Jacobean tragedy — he must try to destroy both the
body and the soul of his victim.[6] For the complete vengeance

----

[6]See Clara F. McIntyre's "The Later Career of the Elizabethan Villain-Hero,"
PMLA 40 (1925): 874-80. She draws attention to the obvious characteristics of
Elizabethan villain-heroes and then makes parallels to the work of Walpole, Rad-
cliffe, Lewis, Byron, and Shelley.

that Tourneur's *The Revenger's Tragedy,* Middleton's *The Changeling*, and Shakespeare's *Hamlet* must demand, it is necessary that hell receive the soul of one's enemy; so when Zastrozzi vows to murder his own father and his half-brother, the motivation involved partakes of a physical and spiritual kind. In this drastic and intense form of commitment, one sees the Gothic hero-villain as an energetic force designed to exceed normal human experience, and all the major events that surround him are mirrors of his dark energies.

Briefly recapitulated, the history of Zastrozzi's revenge begins with the fact that his mother was seduced and then abandoned by Count Verezzi, who thereafter marries another woman. Zastrozzi, the illegitimate issue of the seduction, years later promises his dying mother that he will avenge her shame. Meanwhile, the Count's marriage produces another son, Verezzi, and Zastrozzi's vow then includes patricide and fratricide. Killing the father is a simple matter and actually takes place outside the story's action, but, because the young Verezzi is innocent of any evil act, Zastrozzi's plan for his destruction is much more complicated: Verezzi must be driven to suicide. As Zastrozzi's character unfolds, one sees him as a villain with an understandable, if excessive, cause; though insidious and a murderer, he must also be seen as a self-righteous avenger of his wronged mother. Thus, complexity of motive, intricacy of action, and exaggerated character types are all present in Shelley's first Gothic novel.

Regrettably, his second novel, *St. Irvyne* (1811), is not nearly so easy to summarize as *Zastrozzi*. Distinct problems arise from two irreconcilable plots, loose development of themes, and vague relationships between central characters.[7] My interest here, though, is not to criticize

---

[7]Without explanation to his publisher or anyone else, Shelley simply left out chapters 5 and 6. As some biographers point out, it is probable that he had become so involved with philosophical and political questions by the end of 1810, just before *St. Irvyne* was published, that he lost interest in the novel and hastily patched it together for the printer.

Shelley's craftmanship but, rather, to extract from the novel a refinement on the hero-villain idea and some interesting situations that reappear in later works. The fact that there are three possible hero-villain figures in the novel (Ginotti of the first plot becomes a totally different character called Nempere in the second plot, and Wolfstein, the main figure of the Ginotti section, is a variation on the convention) and overlapping, inconclusive themes of immortality, the triumph of innocence, and the ultimate punishment of uncontrolled passions does not detract from Shelley's growing view of the real value in the Gothic tradition. Part of that value can be noted in the extremities of action that the story reveals.

The first plot opens with Wolfstein standing on a cliff, questioning the meaning of his life and ready to commit suicide. His despair is interrupted by a group of bandits who invite him to join their company. He agrees and thus meets Ginotti (the Rosicrucian). The complex relationship that develops between the two is based on Ginotti's determination to tell his story of sin and suffering and how he obtained the "secret of life." Without relieving himself of the secret, he cannot die; consequently, through various circumstances, including murder, escape, dissipation, and recurring despair, Wolfstein finds himself committed to hear the Rosicrucian's story. The conclusion to the first plot takes place when they finally meet to exchange the secret and both men suddenly die through the intervention of diabolical supernatural forces. All of these extreme and dramatic events are designed to test the physical and psychological possibilities of the leading characters.

Cast as hero-villains, both men are murderers, rebels, and sufferers haunted by deep anguish and guilt. Like Zastrozzi, they possess excessive pride, nobility, and loftiness of character, and carry within themselves an abiding sense of their own doom. Interestingly enough, Halliburton sees them as extensions and refinements of the main figures in Shelley's first novel:

The kinship between this pair on the one hand and
Zastrozzi-Verezzi on the other is striking. The latter pair, I
suggest, are the earlier two taken a step further. Wolfstein (the
spiritual brother of Verezzi) becomes in the process a more
culpable character. While Verezzi's only crime was to have
been born the son of a scoundrel, Wolfstein is a murderer.
Similarly, while Zastrozzi's crime was relatively justified (mur-
der for vengeance), Ginotti's is far greater: he has renounced
God for the gift of unending life.[8]

Given the values of a nineteenth-century Christian society, it
is not difficult to see the radical and dangerous implications
in these two novels, and the threat to conventional values
stems, for the most part, from the particular nature of the
Gothic hero-villain: he is not content merely to disrupt the
human order but also must project his energies against the
divine. His psychology is of the kind that will destroy any-
one, including himself and the idea of God, so that certain
nihilistic tendencies are satisfied.

The involved second plot of *St. Irvyne* is mostly devoted
to a lengthy description of Nempere's (Ginotti) successful
seduction of the gentle, innocent, and exploited heroine,
Eloise de St. Irvyne, who turns out to be Wolfstein's sister.
Shelley's intention might have been to suggest that
Ginotti-Nempere is a corrupting force that seeks to destroy
Wolfstein's soul and his sister's body, but since the novel is
not fully worked out, one can only speculate about the
relationship of the two plots. In any case, the intense pas-
sions that are released through instances of murder, free
love, and revenge directly conform to the interests of the
Gothic tradition.

A further way of understanding the hero-villain is by not-
ing his effect on secondary characters. These characters are
usually manipulated into extreme emotional states through a
course of action that reflects violent, conflicting circum-
stances, which hearkens back to Walpole's notion of "a

---

[8]Halliburton, p. 43.

constant vicissitude of interesting passions." For example, whereas Zastrozzi, Ginotti, and Wolfstein are depicted as melancholic figures who suffer from an internal malaise of mysterious origin, secondary characters, sometimes in combination with the hero-villain, create direct, immediate anguish and terror. Shelley engenders these emotional states by using a series of breathless adventures at the beginning of each novel. In *Zastrozzi*, the young Verezzi is drugged, kidnapped, chained in a cave, and subjected to slow torture. The miraculous intervention of a thunderbolt, which almost kills him, leads to his escape, but he soon falls into Zastrozzi's power once again. To increase the psychological tension, the author portrays a setting for these events that is typically Gothic: mountains, woods, caves, storms, castles, and darkness. The importance of these external features is that they permit us to appreciate the frenzied internal state of the victim and help us to understand a mental reality in terms of a physical one.

A similar atmosphere is provided in the opening paragraph of *St. Irvyne*:

> In this scene, then, at this horrible and tempestuous hour, without one existent earthly being whom he might claim as friend, without one resource to which he might fly as an asylum from the horrors of neglect and poverty, stood Wolfstein;—he gaxed upon the conflicting elements; his youthful figure reclined against a jutting granite rock; he cursed his wayward destiny, and implored the Almighty of Heaven to permit the thunderbolt, with a crash terrific and exterminating, to descend upon his head, that a being useless to himself and to society might no longer, by his existance, mock Him who ne'er made aught in vain.[9]

From these initial dramatic scenes that introduce attempted murder in the first novel and attempted suicide in the second ensue a rapid series of adventures through which the victim

---

[9]*Complete Works*, 5:109.

and lesser characters are guided, by the power of Zastrozzi and Ginotti, to ultimate doom. Verezzi, who loves the innocent Julia, is tricked into marrying Matilda. When Julia suddenly appears on the scene, Verezzi, driven to madness, stabs himself and thus plays completely into Zastrozzi's plan of destroying both his body and his soul. In turn, Matilda takes up Verezzi's dagger and murders Julia. Finally, Zastrozzi and his accomplice, Matilda, are brought before the Inquisition and examined; Matilda repents and is imprisoned, but Zastrozzi remains defiant to the end and dies, mocking God and man, on the rack. And, if anything, the events in *St. Irvyne* are even more intense and dramatic than those in *Zastrozzi*. Wolfstein's involvement with Ginotti, Megalena, and Olympia leads to such sensational adventures that the victim's mind constantly verges on collapse. When Wolfstein is physically and spiritually exhausted, when his mind can no longer stand the frenzy and chaos about him, then the path to his destruction is clear. The deaths of Wolfstein, Megalena, and Ginotti, in the eerie vaults of the castle of St. Irvyne, come as a necessary and dramatic relief to the main action of the novel.

What stands out as significant in the pattern of events depicted in Shelley's two novels is the author's intention of sustaining desperate conflict and uncertainty. The suspense and anguish that surround the hero-villain figures, his victims, and the secondary characters lead to a vortex of destruction that reveals, through violent action, much about the dark side of human nature. "Curiously enough," as one critic explains it,.

the fascination for the bizarre, the individual peculiarity, the monstrous seems to have led more significantly to a fictional discovery of the true depths of human nature than to a mere exploitation of the sensational and the perverse. By its insistence on singularity and exotic setting, the gothic novel seems to have freed the minds of readers from direct involvement of their superegos and allowed them to pursue daydreams and wish fulfilment in regions where inhibitions and guilt could be suspended. Those regions became thereby available to great writers who eventually demonstrated that sadism, indefinite guiltiness, mingled pleasure and pain...and love-hate, were also deeply rooted in the minds of the supposedly normal.[10]

Thus, evil characters and dire situations release much by way of psychological insight, for they inform an audience of its own overt or covert inclinations, its own uncertainties and conflicts. Furthermore, the Gothic novel was one means of providing for a vicarious resolution to man's brutal energies; and the pleasure that derives from being involved with evil, but escaping from it, is of the highest kind. On this point, Halliburton quotes Edmund Burke:

> Whatever is fitted in any sort to excite the ideas of pain and danger, that is to say, whatever is in any sort terrible, or is conversant about terrible objects, or operates in a manner analogous to terror, is a source of the sublime; that is, it is productive of the strongest emotion which the mind is capable of feeling.[11]

Though it would be an ambitious task to prove that Shelley's novels reached the level of the sublime, this, apparently, is what he sought, and we can note this Gothic characteristic now for future reference to such works as *Prometheus Unbound* and *The Cenci*.

Another important characteristic of the Gothic sensibility related to the idea of the sublime is the presence of psychological experience that derives from the distempered mind and that often results in a dream-vision state. Ordinarily, this experience happens only to the victim, and, in the Gothic novel, it becomes a source of objective insight into the character's thoughts. There will be a fuller discussion of this topic in the next chapter; here it is important to show

---

[10]Lowry Nelson, Jr., "Night Thoughts on the Gothic Novel," in *Pastoral and Romance*, ed. Eleanor Terry Lincoln (Englewood Cliffs, N. J., 1969), p. 261.

[11]Edmund Burke, *A Philosophical Enquiry into the Origins of our Ideas of the Sublime and the Beautiful*, ed. J. T. Boulton (New York, 1958), p. 39. Quoted by Halliburton, p. 48. See also Samuel H. Monk, *The Sublime* (London, 1935).

that its initial appearance in Shelley's work is found in the anxious and harried lives of Verezzi and Wolfstein. The basic affliction of both men is developed through a long exposure to contending passions, and in such intensified emotional climates reside visions and truths released, by madness or momentary derangement, from the fetters of the mundane world. For example, after great internal debate as to whether or not he should marry Matilda, Verezzi has a disturbed dream in which he realizes that he loves only Julia and should not align himself with Matilda, who appears as a threatening force. Unfortunately, he ignores this subconscious warning and leads himself to destruction. An even better example of dream experience and its relation to the distraught psyche occurs in *St. Irvyne*. Wolfstein, torn and unstable because of his confrontions with Ginotti and, like Verezzi, his involvement with two women, can find no respite, not even in his sleep. His meetings with Ginotti always take place under forbiding and tense circumstances, and the Rosicrucian's secretive and sinister habits cause such intense fears in the victim's mind that he often suffers from dreadful dreams:

> sleep crept imperceptibly over his senses; yet, in his visions, was Ginotti present. He dreamed that he stood on the brink of a frightful precipice, at whose base, with deafening and terrific roar, the waves of the ocean dashed; that, above his head, the blue glare of the lightning dispelled the obscurity of midnight, and the loud crashing of the thunder was rolled franticly from rock to rock; that, along the cliff on which he stood, a figure, more frightful than the imagination of man is capable of portraying, advanced towards him, and was about to precipitate him headlong from the summit of the rock whereon he stood, when Ginotti advanced and rescued him from the grasp of the monster; that no sooner had he done this, than the figure dashed Ginotti from the precipice — his last groans were borne on the blast which swept the bosom of the ocean. Confused visions then obliterated the impressions of the former, and he rose in the morning restless and unrefreshed.[12]

---

[12]*Complete Works*, 5: 137-38.

The impressive factor in this passage is how certain elements, in dream form, illustrate the features of the delirious mind. The locale, the weather, a monster, a rescuer (who is later responsible for the victim's destruction), murder, and finally a fully awakened state but one that is still hounded by its nightmares — all of these instances can be viewed as objective indices of the chaos that exists in Wolfstein's mind. He is unable to impose order on his confused life, and his dream signals a true inner condition of uncertainty, fear, and spiritual disintegration.

About the nature of dreams, Jung argues that they

> contain images and thought associations which we do not create with conscious intent. They arise spontaneously without our assistance and are representatives of a psychic activity withdrawn from our arbitrary will. Therefore the dream is, properly speaking, a highly objective, natural product of the psyche, from which we might expect indications, or at least hints, about certain basic trends in the psychic process.[13]

The practice of Shelley and many other Gothic writers suggests that they would agree with this observation. What distinguishes their use of dream and vision, though, is the factors of terror, horror, and mystery connected with the lives of certain characters. Thus, the Gothic sensibility often employed the dream as a product of dramatic external action and internally distraught emotions to reveal some objective, psychological truth about a character or a particular situation.

A final topic that we can consider in relation to Shelley's novels, and one that, because of the nature of poetry, will have dramatic importance as this study progresses, is the particular significance of conventional Gothic imagery and trappings. The psychological effect of juxtaposing forests, wild terrains, forbidding ruins and castles, threatening

---

[13]*The Basic Writings of C. G. Jung,* ed. Violet Staub de Laszlo (New York, 1959), p. 112.

weather, and other sense impressions that might induce fear has already been suggested, but the great emphasis that Gothic novelists gave to these surface features insists, finally, that the real issue is one of mood and tone, of atmosphere. Through careful manipulation of physical detail, the Gothic writer attempts to exceed the boundaries of normal sense experience and establish the proper conditions under which the intangible, the mysterious, might flourish. In a recent article, Robert D. Hume indicates that

> the key characteristic of the Gothic novel is not its devices, but its atmosphere. The atmosphere is one of evil and brooding terror; the imaginary world in which the action takes place is the author's objectification of his imaginative sense of the atmosphere. In other words, the setting exists to convey the atmosphere.[14]

Thus, when sinister figures like Zastrozzi and Ginotti, highly emotional, sensitive characters like Verezzi and Wolfstein, strong, passionate women like Matilda and Megalena, and innocent types like Julia and Eloise confront one another in a particular setting, the reader's response to the situation is mainly determined by the atmosphere within which these Gothic creations find themselves. The rustling leaf, a secretive footstep, and strange, dank chambers are valuable devices because of what they permit to happen in a larger context. One soon realizes that trappings and conventional imagery serve physical and psychological reality so that the interplay of selected elements becomes circular and results in a distinct atmosphere: sinister surroundings complement the activity of the villain and encourage him to execute dire deeds, while these same suroundings intimidate the victim and cause him to feel threatened.

Expanding the idea of Gothic imagery and external de-

---

[14]Robert D. Hume, "Gothic versus Romantic: a Revaluation of the Gothic Novel," *PMLA* 84 (1969) :286. In line with Hume's idea, I will use the term *Gothic imagery* or *atmospheric imagery* throughout the study to mean those images that are designed to intimidate and threaten the victim.

vices, then, we note how atmosphere controls the reader's attention and provides the meeting ground for good and evil, for light and dark forces. Insofar as the Gothic novel tries to present these forces in an extraordinary manner, through a unique type of atmosphere, it becomes apparent that bizarre settings are crucial not in themselves but because of their effects. Any definition of the Gothic sensibility cannot avoid the question of imagery and physical circumstance as important factors, for method and meaning are inextricable: one determines the other.

This brief review of *Zastrozzi* and *St. Irvyne* is designed to indicate Shelley's youthful involvement with the Gothic tradition and also to emphasize certain common characteristics of these novels that will have direct bearing on the overall study. I agree that "the pure tale of horror can never reach a high literary standard, because it uses the most primitive devices to create terror, and often merely disgusts where it should frighten."[15] But certainly Shelley's novels, for all their crudities, are more than simply concentrated attemps at distilled horror: it is obvious that his interest in the bold, the rebellious, and the awesome in human experience — either actual (in terms of fiction) or psychological — becomes the starting point for other preoccupations. When terror, horror, and, more significantly, the mind in a state of turbulence mingle with ideas of free love, defiance of man's and God's laws, terrible destructive tendencies, and the ambiguous line between good and evil, then Shelley's novels can be viewed seriously as indicators of his later concerns. Though most of these early ideas appear indirectly or immaturely handled, we find Shelley, at 16 and 17 years of age, striving to express what will later develop as major poetic directions.

At first one might wonder why the exaggerated and dramatic mode of the Gothic tradition became so important for Shelley and for European society in general. What qual-

---

[15]Peter Penzoldt, *The Supernatural in Fiction* (New York, 1965), p. 93.

ities in the tradition answered to the psychological demands that would eventually produce *Alastor, Prometheus Unbound,* and *The Cenci* or Mary Shelley's *Frankenstein,* Byron's *Manfred,* and Goethe's *Faust*? Joyce Tompkins describes these demands well:

> More and more . . . readers of all kinds . . . no longer content with the compensations of sensibility, groped towards the colossal, the impassioned, the dark sublime. They wanted to see great forces let loose and the stature of man once more distended to its full height, even if it were stretched on the rack. They wanted to see him ablaze with destructive fire or tempered by his will to an icy ruthlessness; they wanted to see him stride over the laws of man and affront the laws of God; they wanted vehemence and tumult, and measureless audacity and measureless egoism.[16]

In relatively crude form, the Gothic novel responded fully to the notion of excessive action and passion, physical or spiritual (and preferably a combination of both), and the modern reader recognizes behind the defiant and destructive fabric of the Gothic tradition what we have come to call the "overreacher" pattern: the scenes, characters, and themes are designed to intensify the reader's response so that a new depth of perception can be introduced. It became necessary to exaggerate human possibilities because writers were dissatisfied with the obvious and conventional limitations that society forced upon them. They attempted to go beyond the pedestrian world of human experience to achieve, through the use of terror, horror, and evil, a deeper insight into the mind.

For example, such Gothic conventions as supernatural figures and events, the hero-villain, the innocent victim, and allied interest in violent passions, hubris, revenge, defiance and rebellion, and external conditions that foster gloom, melancholy, and mystery are all means of exceeding the

---

[16]Joyce Tompkins, *The Popular Novel in England 1770-1800* (London, 1932), p. 287.

bonds of probability and plausibility. With this liberty, Shelley and other Gothic novelists hoped to explore certain physical and psychological tendencies toward destruction that might be difficult for an author to portray under more realistic conditions. To be taken seriously, the Gothic tradition must continually be made to face the question of what these writers sought beyond the banal goals of immediate fear and horror. The direction of my argument suggests that some Gothic authors, including Shelley, became interested in this tradition primarily because, as Spacks observes, "if speculation about demons reveals nothing about the nature of the universe, it does reveal something about the nature of man."[17] For someone like Shelley, an avowed sceptic, this comment reminds us that the supernatural, the improbable, and the impossible merely served as convenient means, ultimately, for stripping away various masks that man imposes on his experience. What the Gothic tradition actually offered Shelley was an introduction to particular devices for penetrating the complex and haunted areas of the mind, and given these areas of his youthful attentions, it is no great wonder that Gothic conventions should surround social, political, and philosophical questions raised in his mature poetry. But first it will be helpful to note these conventions at work in another area of his juvenilia.

II

Turning to Shelley's youthful poetic experiments, which were published between the writing of *Zastrozzi* and *St. Irvyne*, it is immediately apparent that many of the topics appearing in the novels also find expression in two volumes of early poetry. Since the first section of this chapter was devoted to introducing catergories through which one can

---

[17]Patricia Meyer Spacks, *The Insistence of Horror* (Cambridge, Mass., 1962), p. 114.

study Gothic characteristics in Shelley's works, my approach to *Original Poetry by Victor and Cazire* (1810) and *Posthumous Fragments of Margaret Nicholson* (1810) will be primarily descriptive.[18] This method will permit the reader to note the persistence of the young writer's involvement with the Gothic tradition and also to see how examples of Gothic poetry fit the same categories as those that were provided for his novels.

Readers of Shelley universally agree that little in the two volumes of poetry would herald the appearance of a poet with a great future. In *Original Poetry*, the elements are those dear to most teenagers: hope, despair, sorrow, love, loneliness, horror, betrayal by friends, and a rousing, rebellious attitude.[19] Cameron's remark that "they are no better and no worse than most adolescent verse"[20] describes the general value of these poems accurately. *Posthumous Fragments*, however, gives a much greater emphasis to social and political themes, and though the volume lacks art, it does inform us of the direction of interest pointing to *Queen Mab*.

Of the seventeen poems and fragments in *Original Poetry*, only three stand out as distinctly part of the Gothic tradition (except to indicate that the Shelleys were familiar with Lewis's work, there can be no legitimate reason to review the plagiarized poem "Saint Edmond's Eve"). Though many of the other poems contain conventional trappings, such as "the drear/passing knell," "skeleton grasp," "yelling ghosts," "midnight storm," and so on, it is not difficult to see that they develop sentimental interests that have little

---

[18]*Original Poetry* was a joint effort of Shelley and his sister Elizabeth. Published in September 1810, the volume was quickly recalled when Shelley's publisher indicated plagiarism from M. G. Lewis's *Tales of Terror and Wonder* (scholars still argue as to whether Shelley or his sister did the plagiarizing). Undaunted by this embarrassing situation, the young poet, under the pseudonym of John Fitzvictor, published *Posthumous Fragments* just two months after *Original Poetry*.

[19]Shelley's first political poem, "The Irishman's Song," written in 1809, should be compared to his essay "An Address to the Irish People," written in 1812.

[20]Cameron, *The Young Shelley*, p. 49.

to do with the objectives of terror, horror, and the supernatural or mysterious, which the Gothic sensibility demands. But these objectives, fortunately, can be found in the three poems "Revenge," "Ghasta; or, The Avenging Demon,"[21] and "Fragment; or, The Triumph of Conscience," which adequately provide a beginning for our distinctive concerns.

Zastrozzi is echoed in the short poem "Revenge," especially since the revenge theme is based on the same set of circumstances in both works. Agnes, Adolphus's lover, introduces the action and the Gothic setting by pleading,

> "Ah! quit me not yet, for the wind
> whistles shrill,
> Its blast wanders mournfully over the
> hill,
> The thunder's wild voice rattles madly
> above,
> You will not then, cannot then, leave
> me my love. —"[22]

As the poem progresses, we find that Adolphus has promised to meet the spirit of Conrad, his deceased half-brother, at the tomb of their ancestors, but only under the condition that he, Adolphus, bring with him the most precious possession he has, which, of course, happens to be Agnes. The resemblance between Adolphus and Verezzi and Agnes and Julia is obvious; moreover, the atmosphere created by storms, graveyards, and the night guarantees the appearance of a Zastrozzilike villain. At the sepulchre, Conrad's spirit soon appears and states the reason for the meeting:

---

[21]The idea of an avenging demon is central in Shelley's poetry and, in diverse form, will appear in almost all of the major works. In refined use, "Ghasta" becomes a version of curse-quest experience.

[22]*The Complete Poetical Works of Percy Bysshe Shelley*, ed. Thomas Hutchinson (London, 1943), ll. 1-4. All further poetry quotations are from this volume and only line numbers will be indicated; however, this source will be cited hereafter as *Poems* when reference is made to a poem's preface or notes.

> "Thy father, Adolphus! was false, false
>   as hell,
> And Conrad has cause to remember it
>   well,
> He ruined my Mother, despised me his
>   son,
> I quitted the world ere my vengeance
>   was done."
>
>   (45-48)

The relationship between Adolphus and Conrad and the motivation for revenge are of the same pattern that developed in Zastrozzi, but in the poem supernatural agencies raise the level of action to a more purely designated mood of horror than that found in the novel: through the aid of dark spiritual forces, Conrad returns from the grave to destroy both the body and soul of his victim, but instead of harming Adolphus directly, the spirit threatens that which is most precious to him — not his body but the life of his beloved Agnes. Again, the revenge must be accomplished through suicide. Thus, as the spirit of Conrad carries Agnes away, in typical Gothic fashion, the mental state of the victims must be one of total horror and despair so that the only acceptable conclusion to the action is one of complete annihilation:

> "Now Adolphus I'll seize thy best loved
>   in my arms,
> I'll drag her to Hades all blooming in
>   charms,
> On the black whirlwind's thundering
>   pinion I'll ride,
> And fierce yelling fiends shall exult
>   o'er thy bride —"
>
>   (53-56)

The contrast here between black and white, evil and good, is designed to shock and horrify the reader: "Hades" instead of bliss will possess the soul of Agnes "all blooming in charms,'' and "fierce yelling fiends,'' instead of Adolphus, will perform the office of the bridegroom.

Admittedly, the emotional content of the poem is not deep, but the sensibility that it purports to explore through an array of Gothic storms, violent passions, charnel houses, innocent victims, ghastly supernatural figures, and grotesque destructive powers[23] interests us much more than Shelley's poetic achievement. Besides psychological tension and a certain ambiguity in our response to Conrad's reason for revenge, the poem hopes to awaken the reader to the terrible dimensions of fear and evil that we associate with the grave; beyond our pity for the innocent victims and the revenge theme, Shelley is focusing on our fascination with death.

The use of Gothic trappings as one way to indicate this fascination continues in "Ghasta; or, The Avenging Demon" (whose story, in large part, comes from an incident in Lewis's *The Monk*; in fact, the refrain " 'Mortal! Mortal! thou must die,' " and the line " 'Thou art mine and I am thine' " are stolen directly from Lewis[24]), but there is a progression toward the more subtle exploitation of these elements that we can investigate. As in "Revenge," Shelley begins with a threatening external setting that warns of impending death:

> Hark! the owlet flaps her wing,
>   In the pathless dell beneath,
> Hark! night ravens loudly sing,

---

[23]See Arthur Clayborough's *The Grotesque in English Literature* (Oxford, 1965), for a full-length study of the complex psychology that underlies grotesque art. The essential point that the study develops is that the grotesque attracts and repels at the same time, and the impulse to create such a phenomenon grows out of the unconscious.

[24]Lewis himself was guilty of plagiarism, according to Tompkins, for she informs us that about two-thirds of *The Monk* was taken, almost word for word, from a German source. See *The Popular Novel*, p. 245, n. 1. Also see A. B. Young, "Shelley and M. G. Lewis," *MLR* 11 (1906): 322-24, which is helpful but not completely accurate on the issue of Lewis's influence on Shelley.

> Tidings of despair and death. —
> Horror covers all the sky,
>   Clouds of darkness blot the moon,
> Prepare! for mortal thou must die,
>   Prepare to yield thy soul up soon —
>
> (1-8)

In words like *pathless*, *blot*, and *yield*, the point of view suggests that the victim suffers from a distempered mind best described as lost, despairing, and verging on collapse. The personification of horror works to cast a pall over the entire scene so that the reader's mind immediately accepts death as the ultimate conclusion to the action. To sustain and reinforce the impression of the first few lines, the poet, in addition to the usual list of external Gothic features, introduces the mysterious figure of the Wandering Jew and the idea of occult science as a device to discover psychological truth, a truth that permits the victim to die.

After the poem's ominous beginning, a warrior appears, trying to flee unseen forces that resemble the wrath of the Furies: the viewpoint focuses directly on the victim of the haunted mind. At an inn he is confronted by an awesome stranger, "his form Majestic, slow his stride," who induces the warrior to tell his tale of distress. It would seem that Shelley uses the confessional situation as a device to raise the element of fear beyond a particular physical confrontation and into a more abstract experience. The warrior's condition derives from weird nightly visits by a phantom from hell who claims him for a lover, and the result is that he suffers constantly, and more internally than externally. After hearing the tale, the strange confessor promises to discover the cause of the warrior's haunting experiences and leads him to a deserted area:

> The Stranger's look was wild and drear,
>   The firm Earth shook beneath his nod —
>
> He raised a wand above his head,

He traced a circle on the plain,
In a wild verse he called the dead,
  The dead with silent footsteps came.

A burning brilliance on his head,
  Flaming filled the stormy air,
In a wild verse he called the dead,
  The dead in motley crowd were there. —

                                                                    (139-48)

Identified by his power to call forth spirits and also by the
light on his forehead — a blazing cross that he must wear
forever as a sign of God's vengeance — the Wandering Jew
summons forth the phantom of Theresa, the warrior's
former lover, and learns why she torments him nightly. Her
response, "My fleeting false Rodolph to claim," states the
revenge theme, at which point the Jew orders her to return to
the nether regions, then turns to Rodolph, commands him to
gaze upon the blazing cross, and, as agonizing pangs of death
overtake the warrior, sentences him to accompany his lover
to the grave.[25]

The distinguishing characteristics that one can emphasize
in this poem — The Wandering Jew, the use of occult sci-
ence, and the distraught mind — raise its impact above that
of the poem "Revenge" primarily because the cause and
effects of terror here, in "Ghasta," say more about the
human situation than they do about supernatural forces: for
the reader, it is more important to see the suffering of the
warrior and to discover its origin than it is to confront spirits
from hell. To satisify our curiosity, Shelley devises a pattern
whereby a human agent, in possession of supernatural pow-
ers, searches out the warrior's affliction; thus the Wandering
Jew becomes an instrument to interpret different realms of

_____

[25]For a general discussion of the Wandering Jew tradition in Gothic literature, see
Montague Summer's *The Gothic Quest*, pp. 226 ff. James Rieger also deals lengthily
with the legend in *The Mutiny Within* (New York, 1967), pp. 51-71. Finally, for a
complete study of Shelley's interest in the tradition, see Grace Calvert Collins,
"Shelley's Treatment of the Legend of the Wandering Jew" (Master's thesis,
University of North Carolina, 1961).

experience, to act as a mediator between this world and another: in effect, he is a type of priest or primitive psychologist who helps Rodolph's distempered mind to see the reasons for its distress. From this viewpoint, the themes of persecution and revenge assume significance primarily because of what they say about the warrior's conscience and its ability to induce haunting visions that require explanation. This particular emphasis receives more development in the last poem to be noted from *Original Poetry*.

"Fragment; or, The Triumph of Conscience" is an incomplete sketch that Shelley also includes in *St. Irvyne,* with very minor differences between the two poems. Commencing with the usual storm scene, the poem in this instance employs external nature to engender a dream state through which the narrator experiences a new self-dimension:

> Unheeded the thunder-peal crashed in
>   mine ear,
> This heart hard as iron was stranger to
>   fear,
> But conscience in low noiseless
>   whispering spoke.
> 'Twas then that her form on the whirl-
>   wind uprearing,
> The dark ghost of the murdered Victoria
>   strode,
> Her right hand a blood reeking dagger
>   was bearing,
> She swiftly advanced to my lonesome abode.—
> I wildly then called on the tempest to
>   bear me!
>
> (12-19)

Both in the novel and in the volume of poetry, the poem breaks off at this point, but, very interestingly, the novel continues with this observation: "Overcome by the wild retrospection of ideal horror, which these swiftly-written lines excited in his soul, Wolfstein tore the paper, on which he had written them, to pieces, and scattered them about him.''[26] As a point of comparison, the warrior in the previous poem suffered from being pursued by his phantom lover, whom we are led to believe is actual, but in "Fragment," the figure of Victoria is the product of a dream. The "ideal horror" that Wolfstein experiences thus becomes the outgrowth of a disturbed conscience: "real" spirits and terrifying situations are not necessary to conjure up "the dark ghost of the murdered Victoria." The agony that Wolfstein undergoes derives from a horrible deed of the past, and the recording of the deed reproduces the Gothic visions that infest his mind. "Fragment" brings us to the conclusion that the effects of evil work on the protagonist's conscience in such a way that they can force him to the same kind of demise as that encountered by Adolphus and Rodolph.

These three poems, then, serve as examples of how a writer can manipulate Gothic elements to investigate the effects of external and internal circumstances on a particular character. Whether actual or purely visionary, the spirits and demons of the Gothic mode generate the passions, mental tensions, and destructive energies that are so congenial to the factor of "ideal horror" sought by Shelley. The question we are left with, of course, is why Gothic writers felt "ideal horror" to be so important. For the answer we seek, it is necessary to keep in mind that horror and the process by which it repeatedly develops deal with the dark and evil side of experience so that deeper perception, a greater awareness of the buried self, is released; such is the case in "Fragment," where the external threats of nature and Wolfstein's guilty conscience interact to give both the character and the reader a keener knowledge of human anguish and the reasons behind its existence.

Of the seven poems contained in the *Posthumous Fragments of Margaret Nicholson*, only two distinctly embody the techniques and sensibility that determine the line of

---

[26]*Complete Works*, 5:115.

Gothic horror, though most of the other poems do use Gothic imagery to establish themes of love, social injustice, and political anarchy.[27] What we can note about the poems "Fragment" and "The Spectral Horseman," however, is that the terror and horror created verge away from that found in *Original Poetry:* Shelley directs his attention less toward terror and horror for their own sake and more toward the consequences of these states, which fact extends and alters the characteristics that appeared in the first volume of poems. To the reader it is obvious that lack of control and motivation interfere with the quality of *Posthumous Fragments*,[28] possibly due to the same impatience that harms *St. Irvyne*, but the two poems selected here do remain in the Gothic mode and will be succinctly treated as further indication of the directions Shelley is taking.

At first glance, "Fragment" appears melodramatic and unable to reflect any depth of emotion, but the external and conventional Gothic signals can be used to probe beneath the poem's surface. The narrator begins with:

> Yes! all is past — swift time has fled away,
> Yet its swell pauses on my sickening mind;

---

[27]*See Cameron, The Young Shelley*, p. 70 and pp. 347-48, n. 75 and White, pp. 92-94 for cursory discussion of the history and significance of *Posthumous Fragments*.

[28]For example, in "War," one of the non-Gothic poems in this volume, Shelley hearkens back to 18th-century techniques of personification, without great success:

> Now o'er the palsied earth stalks giant Fear,
> With War, and Woe, and Terror, in his train;
> List'ning he pauses on the embattled plain,
> Then speeding swiftly o'er the ensanguined heath,
> Has left the frightful work to Hell and Death.
> (68-72)

Overall, the poem's apocalyptic vision neither brings out an impressive image of fear nor does it horrify us. Familiarity with the poetry of Thomson, Collins, Young, and other 18th-century authors indicates to us where Shelley is learning his youthful attempts at personification and abstraction, but he has not yet mastered a unique approach to the practice. See Carlos Baker's "Spenser, the 18th Century, and Shelley's *Queen Mab*," *MLQ* 2 (1942): 81-98 for Shelley's debt to the neo-classical and Spenserian past.

How long will horror nerve this frame of clay?
I'm dead, and lingers yet my soul behind.
Oh! powerful Fate, revoke thy deadly spell,
And yet that may not ever, ever be,
Heaven will not smile upon the work of Hell;
Ah! no, for Heaven cannot smile on me;
Fate, envious Fate, has sealed my wayward
    destiny.

                                        (1-9)

A form of mental immobility, an inability to break the hold of
a "sickening mind," controls the total meaning and objec-
tive of the poem. The idea of time stopped at an evil moment,
of horror destroying the external functions of life and relent-
lessly attacking the internal life of the soul, of heaven com-
pletely oblivious to a plea for help and forgiveness, and of
unshakable fate directing a "wayward destiny" informs us
that the speaker's mind verges on disintegration and that
death will be a welcome relief. This passage further defines
the attitudes of melancholy and despair so typical of the
Gothic sensibility, and as the poem continues with

I sought the cold brink of the midnight surge,
I sighed beneath its wave to hide my woes,
The rising tempest sung a funeral dirge,
And on the blast a frightful yell arose,

                                        (10-13)

we recognize all the signs of a suicidal state that precludes
any alternative but death. The lines that follow are heavily
seeded with terrifying, chaotic images of storms, a meeting
with a maniac, and finally the graveplot of the narrator's
departed lover. Clearly Shelley desires to accentuate the
impassioned, disjointed mental faculties of the speaker that
move fate's victim toward death and not the external fea-
tures that surround him. Distinct from the three poems
selected from *Original Poetry*, "Fragment" does not depend
on physical violence nor external agents of terror and horror,

real or imagined, to reach its objectives; rather, this poem deals solely with the psychic condition that has accepted death before it happens.

A very different kind of poem appears in "The Spectral Horseman," the last poem to be examined from Shelley's juvenilia. Instead of accepting death, a phantom figure, the "champion of Erin," returns from the grave, apparently to free his people from ruthless political oppression. Though the action is incomplete and some of the references are obscure, the central image of the horseman and the theme of resisting tyranny seem to unite Shelley's "graveyard poetry" with the hint of a new direction in his interests.

Possessing some of the Wandering Jew's qualities, the phantom acts as an agent to release and arouse "the tombless ghosts" of the dead, who, we surmise, will rise up in rebellion against the king. Throughout the poem, the "champion of Erin" appears as a mysterious, heaven-defying messenger, and the poet surrounds him with all the natural and supernatural Gothic devices that the tradition demands:

> The phantom courser scours the waste,
> And his rider howls in the thunder's roar
> O'er him the fierce bolts of avenging Heaven
> Pause, as in fear, to strike his head.
> The meteors of midnight recoil from his figure,
> Yet the 'wildered peasant, that oft passes by,
> With wonder beholds the blue flash through his
>   form:
> And his voice, though faint as the sighs of
>   the dead,
> The startled passenger shudders to hear,
> More distinct than the thunder's wildest roar.
>   (37-46)

As in the previous poem, terror and horror are subordinated to an intention that goes beyond the examples from *Original Poetry*. Unlike the previous poem, though, which dealt with the particular and internal workings of the deranged mind, "The Spectral Horseman" employs external imagery to develop a general, a public statement. In the imagery connected with "the fitful blast of the wind," "a yelling vampire," and "death-swimming eyeballs," we soon see that the frightening, destructive tendencies of the Gothic tradition become, in this instance, mere poses to encompass and play host to the central image of the phantom and the poet's theme of rebellion. Seriously worth noting at this juncture is Shelley's willingness to take up a social and political interest and clothe it in Gothic trappings; what takes shape is the fact that Shelley is beginning to exceed the usual confines of terror and horror so that a certain literary mode will serve diverse functions, as occurs in the quoted passsage, for the imagery supports both the "mystic form" of the horseman and the menacing nature of the theme. Fortunately for this study, the two volumes of early poetry contain those external and internal specimens of involvement with the Gothic tradition that will permit one to impose a critical progression leading toward Shelley's mature work, but a final source should be included before we examine *Queen Mab*.

Not published until 1964, about 150 years after the poems were written, *The Esdaile Notebook*[29] handily bridges the divide that many scholars have permitted to exist between the juvenilia and the major poetry of Shelley. Though there appears little in the volume that could contribute significantly to the study of Gothic elements beyond what has already been said, a large number of themes in the *Notebook* form a concentrated prelude to Shelley's first mature achievement: "The poems attack social injustice, political tyranny, and organized religion. They advocate — sometimes directly, sometimes by implication — a democratic republic and a social order based on economic equality, peace, religious tolerance, and civil liberties."[30] (There is

---

[29]*The Esdaile Notebook*, ed. Kenneth Neil Cameron (New York, 1964).
[30]*Ibid.*, p. 5.

also a group of personal poems, which are important primarily for biographical interest.) The *Notebook* is mentioned here mainly because one is struck by Shelley's simultaneous concern with the Gothic tradition and with the themes that Cameron lists. It becomes clear that the revolutionary, unorthodox, and destructive possibilities within the Gothic mode influenced the developing sensibilities of the young poet and also offered him a means to express his growing social and political convictions. Undoubtedly, the preoccupation with defiant figures, heated passions, and dramatic events urges us to see in his juvenilia a seedbed out of which could grow the serious humanitarian and personal issues that would engross him throughout the remainder of his career. More than simply the external trappings of the Gothic tradition, Shelley brought forward into his mature poetry an attitude toward the complexity of human experience that this tradition tried to explore.

III

Scholars generally recognize Shelley's real literary career as beginning with the publication of *Queen Mab*, which appeared in 1813, more than two years after his last "distempered, although unoriginal visions," as he called his Gothic novels, in a letter to Godwin.[31] Since those visions, he had been expelled from Oxford, had entered into a hasty marriage, and had engaged in various political and social activities in Ireland and Wales.[32] And though considered by some Shelley students as quixotic and juvenile actions, all of them, including his marriage, have at their center the ques-

---

[31]*Complete Works*, 8: 287. For other letters on the early novels and poetry see pp. 4-5, 6, 18, 7-10, and 19.

[32]Shelley's commitment to Irish freedom is fully discussed in Cameron's *The Young Shelley*, pp. 148-79. Cameron destroys the popular image of a naïve Shelley going off to fight windmills, and shows him to be an insightful political observer. In general, contemporary scholarship is paying increasing respect to Shelley's social and political acumen, especially when his mature poetry is compared with his essays, particularly an essay like "A Philosophical View of Reform."

tion of freedom and tyranny: Shelley was expelled from Oxford not because he wrote "The Necessity of Atheism" but because he refused to say that he did not write it; he married Harriet Westbrook, as the accumulated evidence of White and Cameron indicates, not so much out of deep love but more out of the belief that she was the victim of an oppressive home and school situation; and last, the plight of the suppressed Irish and the destitute Welsh peoples played its part in awakening his humanitarian impulses. Thus, many of the ideas in *Queen Mab* that form the argument against tyranny and injustice are drawn, in some measure, from personal experience as well as from reading and reflection.[33] Furthermore, the poem conveniently employs certain literary devices that arose out of our survey of his early work and, in a general way, displays many of the essential directions that Shelley will follow for the remaining nine years of his life.

When one examines elements in *Queen Mab* that reflect the Gothic tradition, it is misleading on the basis of a few conventions to call the work a Gothic poem. Above all else, it is a revolutionary poem — one that attacks commonly accepted political, religious, and materialistic enterprises, both past and present, and then offers a vision of the perfect future state that will result from the overthrow of tyrannical forces:

> His ideological argument includes a historical survey of human misery and crime; a series of allegations against superstitition and Christian dogma as the sources of much of that misery and criminality; a pseudo-deistic rejection of the concept of God as an anthropomorphic Being, and as the type of vengeful ruler who must be propitiated by sacrifice, prayer, and genuflexion; and a pantheistic argument for the existence of a Nature-Spirit, Shelley's substitute for the traditional Christian deity. Finally

---

[33]Carl Grabo's *The Magic Plant* (Chapel Hill, N. C. , 1939) also states the case for Shelley's realistic approach to political freedom and reform (see especially pp. 422-32), but Grabo's "Nursling of Revolt" discussion leads the reader toward neo-platonic conclusions that Cameron will not readily accept.

he indulges the optimistic, progressivistic, and in one sense idealistic supposition that at a future date the normal operations of the Nature-Spirit will have produced widespread climatic changes in the world, and that these changes (owing to psycho-physical connections) will be reflected in the realms of morals and general human welfare.[34]

Given this basic statement of theme, one must immediately accept particular limitations on the role of Gothic components in the poem: there occurs no overriding motif of horror or terror (except insofar as one considers the whole history of needless human suffering as horrible, which Shelley did), and there prevails a primary intellectual and didactic intention that, at best, remains secondary in most Gothic literature. Nonetheless, such features as the dream-vision technique, Gothic imagery, the legend of the Wandering Jew, the story of an atheist, and a few minor characteristics from Shelley's early work become central to the poem's thematic development.

Queen Mab opens with lines that remind us of poems from Shelley's juvenilia:

How wonderful is Death,
Death and his brother Sleep!
One, pale as yonder waning moon
With lips of lurid blue. . . .

(I. 1-4)

Rather than to create a mood of fear, though, "Death," "Sleep," and "lips of lurid blue" are designed to introduce a mood of mystery, of suspense, of the exotic so that the poet's true purpose can be achieved quickly — that is, to locate the action of the poem outside of normal human experience and to place the scene in an imaginary sphere. The spirit of the sleeping Ianthe must be free to enter the magic car of the Fairy Queen and be whisked away to a

---

[34]Carlos Baker, *Shelley's Major Poetry* (Princeton, 1948), p. 37.

celestial realm where the panorama of the past, present, and future condition of mankind can be revealed.

To satisfy his intention, Shelley chooses a dream-vision as the most convenient technique to present metaphysical experience. Earlier we noted its use and effect in *Zastrozzi*, *St. Irvyne*, and *Posthumous Fragments* to produce comparable extraterrestrial or psychic events, and Shelley was certainly familiar with the dream-vision device in Lewis's *The Monk*, Dacre's *Zofloya*, and Godwin's *St. Leon*, to say nothing of Volney's *Les Ruines* (which many commentators say is the source for *Queen Mab*).[35] As seen previously, freeing the spirit or the mind from the confines of the body, from physical reality, the dream-vision permits Wolfstein to confront psychically the ghost of Victoria, and Verezzi to intuit the nature of his love for Matilda.

In *Queen Mab*, however, the visionary technique served Shelley in two distinct ways, neither of which can be termed truly Gothic because they seek ends that are loftier than the Gothic tradition will normally allow. The first condition that the dream-vision establishes in the poem is an omniscient viewpoint; thus the impression of absolute truth is guaranteed. Its second major function is to create a natural mask to investigate and question conventional political and religious practices that might be dangerous to attack directly.[36] When Queen Mab informs Ianthe's spirit of the long and brutal

---

[35]Of course, dream and vision are common characteristics in the work of Homer, Virgil, Dante, Spenser, Shakespeare, Milton and many other authors Shelley knew well, but what is particularly noticeable about the Gothic dream-vision is that it usually haunts, drives, and menaces, and arises from some such forbidding place as a castle, a graveyard, or a wild natural area.

[36]Tompkins indicates the basis for caution: "At the end of the eighteenth century, rumours of secret societies and widespread conspiracies flew thick. Great changes were in progress, and men of liberal sympathies and men tenacious of ancient forms of life were alike prone to see something monstrous and abnormal in each other's activities" (pp. 281-82). Shelley himself was under surveillance by the British government immediately after his return from Ireland; and we cannot be unmindful of the political, social, and religious unrest that pervaded much of Europe in the late eighteenth and early nineteenth centuries that jeopardized a reactionary government and church. Also see Mrs. Shelley's "Note on *Hellas*," in *Poems*, p. 480.

history of monarchical and political oppression (Cantos II-V) and of the hypocritical and cruel behavior of religious institutions (Cantos VI-VII), one realizes that Shelley has used again, but altered, a common Gothic device that allows an escape from the rational, pedestrian world of normal human experience so that the reader can enter a supersensory, multi-dimensional world of the mind. The poet's intention, though, is not to flee from reality but to go more deeply into it:

> "I am the Fairy Mab: to me 'tis given
> The wonders of the human world to keep:
> The secrets of the immeasurable past,
> In the unfailing consciences of men,
> . . . .
> And it is yet permitted me, to rend
> The veil of mortal frailty, that the spirit,
> Clothed in its changeless purity, may know
> How soonest to accomplish the great end
> For which it hath its being, and may taste
> That peace, which in the end all life will
> share."
>
> (I.167-85)

Mab's revelations can occur only while Ianthe is in a state of trance and her spirit receptive to the instruction given her, for the deepest intuitions of man, according to the poem's logic, come during moments of release from finite bondage. Unquestionably, Shelley employs the qualities of the dream state to achieve a form of oracular power, and through this power, he can present those abstractions, those deep visions of intense human consciousness, that will remain his principal concerns in the major poetry from *Queen Mab* to "The Triumph of Life": "the unfailing consciences of men," "the veil of mortal frailty," "changeless purity" (meaning the ideal state), and "peace." As is proper, Shelley approaches abstraction on its own terms, on the level of metaphysical experience. But there are other concerns — entirely negative — that also appear in the visionary realm, and, as one might anticipate, the poet drapes their dark, evil intent with Gothic attire.

In his general survey of political oppression,[37] Shelley first surrounds the appearance of Queen Mab with such conventional Gothic imagery as "tainted sepulchres" (I.10), "a lonely ruin" (I.47), and "a visioned ghost" (I.163), so that an atmosphere where strange, secret forces can exist is introduced, and out of this atmosphere the Gothic impulse develops further. The best instances of this development can be seen when the Fairy Queen permits Ianthe to overlook the terrors and horrors of human history, for here the imagery becomes more intense and changes to "the ghost of Freedom" (II.169), "fevered brain" (III.58), "frenzied eye" (III.63), "Lowered like a fiend, drank with enraptured ear / The shrieks of agonizing death" (III.182-83), "cold and bloody shroud" (IV.48), "the frantic wail of widowed love / Comes shuddering on the blast" (IV.55-56), and "their bones / Bleaching unburied in the putrid blast" (IV.86-87). Through such particular and gruesome images, Mab portrays those destructive, evil conditions that exactly oppose the "changeless purity" that might pervade man's life if he would cease to hate: because man insists on tyrannizing other men, freedom has become only a ghost that surveys scenes of carnage, chaos, and death. Here the Gothic mode dramatically satisfies one of the two polar situations that Shelley needs to formulate the logic of his argument.

By manipulating Gothic imagery, Shelley attemps to describe the process by which a comparatively small group of men consistently exploit the energies and well-being of a much larger group. Beyond the humiliation and degradation of the human body and spirit, however, what the poet sees as

---

[37]Both Ivan Roe, *Shelley: The Last Phase* (London, 1953), pp. 102ff. and Seymour Reiter, *A Study of Shelley's Poetry* (Albuquerque, N. M., 1967), p. 48 tend to deal with the poet's political consciousness from the viewpoint of practical idealism. The strain of eighteenth-century rationalism that pervades much of *Queen Mab* (especially apparent in the "Notes" to the poem) later changes to the idealism of *Prometheus Unbound*.

the most fearsome condition of existence is the complete loss of freedom for oppressor and victim alike; as a system of political and social rule, tyranny demands that masters and slaves live in common bondage to hate, suspicion, and fear:

> . . . for kings
> And subjects, mutual foes, forever play
> A losing game into each other's hands,
> Whose stakes are vice and misery. The man
> Of virtuous soul commands not, nor obeys.
> Power, like a desolating pestilence,
> Pollutes whate'er it touches; and obedience,
> Bane of all genius, virtue, freedom, truth,
> Makes slaves of men, and, of the human frame,
> A mechanized automaton.
>
> (III.171-80)

This clearly didactic portion of the poem rises partially out of Shelley's Gothic background and even reminds us of some circumstances in the early works: recalling the tyrant-victim relationship of Zastrozzi and Verezzi in Shelley's first novel and of Ginotti and Wolfstein in his second, one notes that *Queen Mab* has simply expanded the focus of the oppressor-oppressed idea so that the psychological dimension of those four characters takes on universal proportions. It is not simply that individuals persecute one another but that whole societies engage in the practice also. Slowly the poet's "distempered visions" are maturing into a broader conception, with conventional Gothic imagery helping to bring out the "dark" aspects of this conception. Moreover, when the poem turns to attack religion, it depends particularly on types of Gothic characters to make its point.

Just as Shelley's hero-villain Zastrozzi defied the religious inquisition that finally put him to death — "Even whilst writhing under the agony of almost unsupportable torture. . . Zastrozzi's firmness failed him not; but, upon his soul-illumined countenance, played a smile of most disdainful

scorn . . .''[38] — so, too, Ianthe's spirit recounts an incident
of similar import:

"I was an infant when my mother went
To see an atheist burned. She took me there:
The dark-robed priests were met around the pile;
The multitude was gazing silently;
And as the culprit passed with dauntless mien,
Tempered disdain in his unaltering eye,
Mixed with a quiet smile, shone calmly forth;
The thirsty fire crept round his manly limbs;
His resolute eyes were scorched to blindness
    soon;
His death-pang rent my heart! the insensate mob
Uttered a cry of triumph, and I wept.
'Weep not, child!' cried my mother, 'for that man
Has said, There is no God.' "

(VII.1-13)

In these examples from the novel and the poem, the temporal
forces of religion act to control and suppress dissident ele-
ments, those who would question the law imposed on the
majority of people. Certainly, the figure of the proud, defiant
Gothic villain perfectly suits Shelley's interest in exposing
the intolerant and vindictive attitudes behind the historical
development of European religious institutions. Involved as
he is with conventionally regarded evil agents, the hero-
villain is a natural choice to oppose tyrannical religious
views and, of course, to be crushed by them: the rebellious
Zastrozzi and the atheist of *Queen Mab*, with whom the
reader is finally led to sympathize, must be sacrificed to
God's representatives. For the man who would challenge
divine force directly, though, Shelley sees in store an even
more terrible fate than death.

Before Queen Mab conjures up the phantom of the Wan-
dering Jew, Ahasuerus, her omniscience — which gives

---

[38]*Complete Works*, 5: 103.

access to, and therefore becomes, the standard of truth in the poem — confirms the belief of the atheist that "there is no God," and the force that men have mistaken for God and imbued with their own tendencies is really the

> "Spirit of Nature! all-sufficing Power,
> Necessity! thou mother of the world!"
>
> (VI.197-98)

But because man refuses to live in accordance with the harmonious laws of nature and because he insists on inventing and perpetuating the image of an anthropomorphic God, his destiny is one of self-imposed suffering and servitude.

Ahasuerus is just such a victim, for Mab refers to him as

> ". . . a wondrous phantom, from the dreams
> Of human error's dense and purblind faith, . . ."
>
> (VII.64-65)

A perfect example (and a favorite with the Romantic writers in general) of the long-suffering, proud, and hounded seeker of physical and spiritual peace, he longs for a release that can come only through death, which, because of divine wrath, is forever denied to him. His painful existence metaphorically states the condition of the human consciousness that needlessly accepts a fate it neither deserves nor, except for false guilt, has to accept. When Ianthe asks the Jew if there is a God, he replies,

> "Is there a God! — ay, an almighty God,
> And vengeful as almighty!"
>
> (VII.84-85)

Ahasuerus then proceeds to recount the biblical story of creation, the fall of man, the coming of a savior, and finally how the Jew mocked Christ at the crucifixion, which resulted in his being condemned to eternal life and wandering.

In the same way that the atheist resembles Zastrozzi, so Ahasuerus appears as an extension of Ginotti, but in *Queen Mab* the legend varies and the Wandering Jew becomes a chronicler of the human misery that has resulted from religious wars and persecution undertaken in the name of God. The finer point that Shelley makes through the proclamation of the Fairy Queen, however, insists that God's existence and eternal ire are merely products of the Jew's imagination: he is guilty of nothing but "human error's dense and purblind faith." Nonetheless, his false beliefs and unwarranted feelings of guilt imprison him as truly as do the religious institutions that burn the atheist.

A terrible irony begins to take shape in the false punishment meted out to the atheist and to the Jew: according to Queen Mab, the atheist is right that there is no God, and he must burn for his insight, while the Jew is wrong in thinking that there is a God, and he also must suffer for his beliefs. One can see these two victims as symbolic projections of an evil and oppressive religious climate. Doubtless Shelley would agree with Nietzsche's notion of "the slave mentality" and with his analysis of the brutal and insidious pattern by which man is externally (through institutions) and internally (through the guilty conscience) controlled.[39] Little does it matter whether one is an atheist or an Ahasuerus, one who does not believe in God or one who does; what concerns Shelley is the subtle tactic by which men, here represented by two types of Gothic figures, are subjugated.

Further discussion of *Queen Mab* would have to include an analysis of the principle of Necessity[40] as a viable substitute for the idea of God and an account of the principle of

---

[39]Friedrich Nietzsche, *The Philosophy of Nietzsche* (New York, n.d.). Relative to this point is "The Genealogy of Morals."

[40]*Poems*, "Notes on Queen Mab," pp. 809-12, contains Shelley's own statement on Necessity.

Perfectibilitarianism,[41] which Shelley, primai ily through the study of Godwin's *Political Justice*, thought would direct mankind toward a happier future state, but such issues cannot aid, in any direct way, the study of Gothic elements in the poem. Instead, this discussion of *Queen Mab* can best close by recalling that the poem does carry on Shelley's involvement with the Gothic tradition through such relevant features as the refined use of the dream-vision, a type of imagery common to that tradition, and certain hero-villain figures. In diverse ways, these characteristics serve Shelley's larger intention of dealing with the serious theme of political and religious tyranny. Furthermore, it is logical that the Gothic world of rebellion, anguish, and terror should lead the poet to incorporate many of its themes and psychological particularities into the world of *Queen Mab*, which can be viewed as a natural outgrowth of Shelley's literary and personal history as well as the first major step toward his mature poetry.

The following chapters will test the principal emphasis that we have given to the Gothic tradition apparent in Shelley's early work. I concur with the statement of Hal-

---

[41]Much has been written about Shelley's naive vision of utopia and of the likelihood of man's perfectibility, but it is a gross misunderstanding both of Shelley and of perfectibility that accounts for most of the criticism. Shelley agreed with the following statement by Godwin: "By perfectible, it is not meant that he [man] is capable of being brought to perfection. But the word seems sufficiently adapted to express the faculty of being continually made better and receiving perpetual improvement; and in this sense it is here to be understood. The term perfectible, thus explained, not only does not imply the capacity of being brought to perfection, but stands in express opposition to it. If we could arrive at perfection, there would be an end to our improvement. There is however one thing of great importance that it does imply: every perfection or excellence that human beings are competent to conceive, human beings, unless in cases that are palpably and unequivocally excluded by the structure of their frame, are competent to attain." William Godwin, *Enquiry Concerning Political Justice*, in *Backgrounds of Romanticism*, ed. Leonard M. Trawick (Bloomington, Ind., 1967), p. 202. Obviously, there is nothing naïve about this rational argument and the qualified utopian scheme that it suggests. For a typical example of misinterpreting and blurring Shelley's idea of perfection, however, one should see Edward Bostetter's *The Romantic Ventriloquists* (Seattle, Wash., 1963), p. 217.

liburton that "from the preoccupation with ideas and spirits and phantoms in the novels to the world of *Prometheus Unbound* is really not such a long step"[42] and with that of Benjamin Kurtz that Shelley's interest in death, ghosts, and terror forms a link between his juvenilia and his mature work:

> the predisposition is notable, and in the absence of a precise explanation of it we must continue to speak of it somewhat spectrally as a special affinity for the metaphysical. We may not be so very far wrong if in this buoyant, extravagant play in the graveyard we detect the first crude, bizarre symptom of an as yet undeveloped gift for seeing the invisible.
>
> Indeed, there is a striking, even if remote, parallel between these boyish ghost-hunts, and that sustained impressibility toward the mysterious conditions of man's life that characterized Shelley's mature thought and lay at the source of his greatest symbolic creations.[43]

Certainly the Gothic tradition offers us the sense of the metaphysical and invisible that Kurtz suggests, but this work from here on will stress the viewpoint that these are projections of the creative imagination aimed at interpreting and presenting "the mysterious conditions of man's life." Imaginatively, Shelley keeps one eye on the world beyond so that he can more clearly see into this one. To indicate how he relates the two is the theme of the following chapters.

42Halliburton, p. 49.

43Benjamin Kurtz, *The Pursuit of Death* (London, 1933), p. 7.

2
Gothic Elements in *Alastor*

More completely than any other mature poem in the Shelley canon, *Alastor* serves as a prime example of serious and sophisticated application of character, situation, theme, and mood that derive from the Gothic tradition. The story of an idealistic young poet haunted by a vision of the unattainable and whose quest for it leads him to an early death offered Shelley the opportunity to portray a state, as he termed it, "allegorical of one of the most interesting situations of the human mind."[1] The precise nature of this situation has caused much tedious argument and confusion among Shelley scholars,[2] but understanding the allegory in terms of the Gothic mode should eliminate the major confusion and also further establish categories for examining poems written after *Alastor*.

The dispute over the meaning of the poem derives from the difficulty Shelley students have had in reconciling the preface with the apparent ambiguities the poem presents. Shelley writes that "the Poet's self-centered seclusion was

---

[1]*The Complete Poetical Works of Percy Bysshe Shelley*, ed. Thomas Hutchinson (London, 1943), p. 14. All uncited quotations in this chapter come from Shelley's "Preface" to the poem, pp. 14-15.

[2]See Carlos Baker, *Shelley's Major Poetry*, (Princeton, 1948), pp. 42-47 for a succinct review of scholarship on the poem and for Baker's own position, which I hold to be questionable.

avenged by the furies of an irresistible passion pursuing him to speedy ruin." Most readers have ignored this idea or said that Shelley was merely trying to justify his title *"Alastor*; or, the Spirit of Solitude,"* and, as often noted, "Alastor" means an avenging demon. They thus find the poem's central meaning in the quest motif and largely discount the curse motif that Shelley suggests. If, however, we examine the pattern whereby the poem aligns with Shelley's Gothic period and his use of the curse and quest motifs, the preface and the poem's allegory can be reconciled, for the logic of this argument insists that quest and curse are, in the poem, intricately bound together and both motifs are needed to determine the poem's meaning. Such Gothic conventions as the hero-villain figure, the dream-vision, atmospheric imagery, and personification provide relationships within the poem that should clearly indicate Shelley's intention. Before dealing directly with *Alastor*, I must define these conventions more completely than was done in the previous chapter.

In *"Alastor* Foreshadowed in *St. Irvyne,"* an article referred to earlier, Jones alerts us to the fact that, up to a point, the story of the hero-villain Ginotti parallels the history of the protagonist in *Alastor*.[3] Though they are handled cursorily, the article compares the poem and the novel along the lines of an obsession with an abiding passion, moral and intellectual ambiguity, gloom, anguish, and melancholy. Throughout my discussion of the poem, these mental states will be analyzed for the purpose of viewing the hero-villain as a complex creation who, on the one hand, deserves our sympathy and, on the other, requires our censure. A major consideration that one must keep in mind, however, is that Shelley's view of the hero-villain figure has altered significantly and lost many of its common Gothic features. A primary factor that helps account for this change and one

---

[3]In another article on this poem, it is ironic that Jones fails to relate the Gothic elements in *Alastor* to Shelley's overall intention and thus falls into the same pattern of confusion that has afflicted most scholars. See F. L. Jones, "The Inconsistency of Shelley's *Alastor*," *ELH* 13 (1946): 291-99.

that affects all the mature poems is Shelley's emphasis on the means whereby the mind determines reality, the type of interchange between external and internal experience. For example, the reader must keep in mind that the conventional religious moral order within which Ginotti appears is very different from the order of nature and purely human context that surrounds the Poet-protagonist in *Alastor*: the former is realistic and straightforward, while the latter is psychologically oriented and extremely complex. In the four years that separate the two works, Shelley has progressed from the simple, external order of Gothic morality to the intricate, internal experiences of the mind, and though Ginotti and the Poet share the curse-quest situation, Shelley's refinement of the convention requires us to raise the hero-villain idea to the level of mental action.

Another element that relates to the Gothic tradition we will seek in *Alastor* is visionary experience, for in the poem the dream-vision feature serves as an involved vehicle for going beyond everyday reality and probing psychic phenomena. Noted earlier in this study was the penchant of Gothic novelists to foreshadow critical events and to indicate the truth about a person or an object by employing the dream-vision. Varma comments on this practice as follows:

> The writers who rediscovered the nebulous world of the supernatural described it as grotesque and nightmarish because that is how, unconsciously, they reacted to unfamiliar passions. Encouraged by their classical education to put aside barbaric emotions and ultradiurnal contemplation, now that upsurging currents of new thought revealed unfamiliar spheres, they were compelled to approach the speculations surreptitiously in dreams, for that was the only way they could achieve super-reality.[4]

Though not wholly applicable to this discussion, Varma's

---

[4]Devendra P. Varma, *The Gothic Flame* (London, 1957), p. 38. Further along the author refers to dreams as "that realm of mysterious subconsciousness which flows eternally like some dark underground river beneath the surface of human life" (p. 80).

speculation that "unfamiliar passions" can lead to dreams that try to state a truth beyond normal experience is solidly embedded in the Gothic tradition. Precisely what one finds in the novels of Walpole, Radcliffe, Lewis, Godwin, Dacre, Shelley, and Maturin is, through dreams or visions, a bold maneuver to pierce appearances and inform the character concerned, and the reader, of a metaphysical or psychological reality. A typical example is found in Charlotte Dacre's *Zofloya*, which was a major influence on Shelley's *Zastrozzi* and *St. Irvyne* and which contains processes applicable to *Alastor*.

After a series of exhausting and gruesome adventures, the novel's female protagonist reflects on Zofloya, who is really Satan disguised as a Moorish servant, before she falls asleep. Then in a dream,

> she beheld a beautiful and seraphic form approach. — When it came near, it seemed to her that her eyes could not sustain the exceeding brilliancy which shot from the countenance, the hair, and the garments of this celestial vision.
>
> "Victoria!" it pronounced in a sweet and awful voice, "I am thy good genius; I come to warn thee at this moment, because it is the first, for many years, in which a spark of repentance hath visited thy guilt-benighted soul. — The Almighty, who wishes to save his creatures from destruction, permits that I appear before thee. — If thou wilt forsake, even yet, the dark and thorny path of sin, if thou wilt endeavour, by thy future life, to make amends for the terrible list of the past, even yet shalt thou be saved! — But above all, thou must fly the Moor Zofloya, who is not what he seems."
>
> At that instant, Victoria saw beneath the feet of the resplendent vision, the Moor Zofloya — he lay prostrate — stripped of his gaudy habiliments, and appearing monstrous and deformed! — Still she recognized him for Zofloya.[5]

A number of situations occur here that repeatedly mainifest themselves in the dream-vision of the Gothic tradition: first,

---

[5]Charlotte Dacre, *Zofloya, or The Moor* (London, 1928), p. 239.

the dreamer is at a climactic, emotion-filled point in her (or his) history; second, a warning or advice of some kind comes through the appearance of a supernatural figure or event; third, the true nature of a character or situation is revealed, though often in obscure fashion; and last, the dreamer and the reader are left in confusion to puzzle out the haunting possibilities of the dream. In Gothic romance, dreams seldom alter anything drastically, but they do inform the reader, with his overview of the story, about the probable outcome of events and about the weaknesses and self-deceptions of the characters involved.

The implications of visionary experience lead one to make certain assumptions about its value: when we attempt to define and analyze Shelley's use of the dream-vision, which is so central to his total work,[6] the clearest way to view it is as a psychic state in which the mind is freed from its common inhibitions and allowed to project its subconscious desires — for good or evil. Since dream-visions give this liberty, they can act as objective devices — as Jung's earlier statement suggests — to determine subconscious truth that is denied when one is awake and mindful of the need to mask his desires, or, from another viewpoint, unable to formulate his desires because they originate from very personal and ideal circumstances, as is the case with the Poet in *Alastor*. The

---

[6]To my knowledge, every major scholar and critic of Shelley has dealt with the problem of visionary experience in his poetry. Some of the critical works that have been very helpful to this study of *Alastor*, in terms of the dream-vision and the allegory, are the following: Baker, *Shelley's Major Poetry*, pp. 41-60; Peter Butter, *Shelley's Idols of the Cave* (Edinburgh, 1954), pp. 47-55; W. H. Hildebrand, *A Study of Alastor* (Kent, Ohio), *KSUB* 42 no. 11 (1954) :18-22, 36, and 46-64; H. L. Hoffman, *An Odyssey of the Soul* (New York, 1933), chap. 2; Albert Gérard, "*Alastor*, or the Spirit of Solipsism," *PQ*, 33 (1954): 164-77; Neville Rogers, *Shelley At Work* (Oxford, 1956), pp. 69-70 ff.; and Earl L. Schulze, *Shelley's Theory of Poetry* (The Hague, 1966), pp. 76-82. Ordinarily, Shelley has been studied either as a poet of Platonism and neoplatonism or as a poet of rationalism—the purely human with regard to psychology and the creative imagination. Though my study does not pay exclusive attention to any one philosophic approach to Shelley's poetry, it will become apparent that the latter suits the demands of my argument more completely than the former. The reason for a rational and psychological approach is that, in the face of Shelley's obvious scepticism, the Gothic tradition answers primarily to basic human concerns and not, as Platonism would (except symbolically), to other worldly interests.

point Shelley wishes to make is that when visionary knowledge is transferred over into waking life, when one tries physically to enact what was originally dream experience, the results bespeak disaster. Ultimately, my analysis of the poem will argue that the ambiguous nature of the Poet's dream-visions is precisely the means by which Shelley develops ambivalent attitudes toward his Poet-hero in *Alastor*.

I do not wish to belabor the point about visionary events in the poem,[7] but this study depends heavily on a proper explanation of them. Furthermore, they help us understand the technical problem Shelley faced when he portrays the workings of the Poet's mind in various stages of development, ecstasy, dissolution, and extinction, for the Poet is first exposed to external phenomena and then dream-visions are employed to reveal the effects of those phenomena on his mind.[8] Finally, to maintain consistency with the Gothic hero-villain tradition just indicated, extensive discussion of the dream-visions will claim that their significance and that of the allegory are exactly in accordance with the curse-quest theme stated in the poem's preface; that is, when one becomes oblivious to love and human sympathy because of an obsession with an ideal—any ideal—then a lonely death is his doom. We may pity the Poet but we must also be critical of him.

Atmospheric imagery and personification are the final elements to note in this prefatory comment on *Alastor*. Par-

---

[7]Altogether, the words *dream* and *vision* are used at least thirteen times in *Alastor*—more than in any other Shelley poem (F. S. Ellis, *A Lexical Concordance to the Poetical Works of Percy Bysshe Shelley* (London, 1892), pp. 181 and 761). Shelley's aforementioned intention of presenting an allegory of the mind helps account for the strong reliance on dream-visions.

[8]A certain caution must be exercised in distinguishing dream-vision experience from other experience. Certainly no invidious distinction will be made through the use of the word *reality*. This study views all of man's experience, dreaming or waking, as "real," and the difference that will be entertained is determined by which state of experience is under discussion. We cannot call a dream "unreal" experience if we agree that experience is that which happens to us; rather, we should view dream experience as different from but equivalent to waking experience.

ticular observations about these elements and Shelley's special use of them must be included at this juncture, especially since they will later relate to the Gothic tradition and clarify the intention in the poem.

Henry Sweet, in an essay that points out what a close student of nature Shelley was, and why, explains that

> Shelley's love of the changing and fleeting aspects of nature — the interest with which he watched the formation of mist and cloud, and the shifting hues of dawn and sunset — is, like his sense of structure, a natural result of the half scientific spirit with which he regarded nature, for it is in the changing phenomena of nature that her real life lies. . . . The most effective way of dealing poetically with the forces of nature is, of course, to personify them.[9]

With our attention called to the fact that Shelley was extraordinarily conscious of natural phenomena and the necessity of personifying them to achieve certain ends, it is worthwhile to note Mrs. Spacks's statements, in *The Insistence of Horror:*

> The personification was by this time [the end of the eighteenth century] a rhetorical device so hallowed by tradition that its limitations and its possibilities were well defined; they clearly left room for Furies and demons, which needed only slight disguise to be contained within the proper rhetorical bounds. And the tension implicit in the technique of using such beings simultaneously for imaginative, moral, and rhetorical effect might be expected to produce a rich and fruitful sort of poetry.[10]

Furthermore, she holds that personification has as its central aim the ability to clarify and emphasize experience; there-

---

[9]Henry Sweet, "Shelley's Nature-Poetry," in *The Shelley Society's Papers*, ser. I, no. 1, pt. II (London 1891), p. 296. The essay interestingly connects Shelley's nature poetry with primitive Hindu poets and with scientific concerns of ancient and modern poetry. Shelley's interest in science is also developed in Carl Grabo's *A Newton Among Poets* (Chapel Hill, N. C., 1930) and *Prometheus Unbound* (Chapel Hill, N. C., 1935).

[10]Patricia Meyer Spacks (Cambridge, Mass., 1962), p. 202.

fore, its purpose is to illuminate rather than to decorate a poem. Sweet and Spacks agree that nature is able to inform man of his moral responsibilities because it embodies mysterious powers for good or evil whose laws man must attempt to fathom through the assistance of his imagination. Thus, in Shelley's case, when nature mirrors or directs the operations of the mind, imagery usually serves as an informative device for mental states. Finally, Peter Butter describes Shelley's two principal methods for examining the intricacies of the mind:

> First, he often represents feelings or states of mind symbolically by means of images of material things. The mind may be a wilderness with many paths or a cave with many chambers, or, more commonly, it may be a whole landscape with cave, tower, streams, whirlpools, woods, etc. Secondly, he sometimes personifies feelings as spirits, demons or other mythical beings.[11]

If one keeps in mind that personification was a rhetorical device firmly established by Shelley's time, that it was a means to deal with forces of nature that affect man in very subtle ways, and that Shelley depends on images and personifications to portray mental sensations, then one more readily sees how certain imagery — which is relatable to the Gothic sensibility—becomes crucial for definite moral, emotional, and intellectual positions. This proposition is especially pertinent when the imagery tends to be directed toward metaphysical interests such as the ideal or death. As we shall soon see, imagery and personification in *Alastor* and in most of Shelley's other poetry are designed for subtle psychological insight. With these introductory observations before us, one can begin an analysis of Gothic elements in *Alastor*, dealing first with the idea of the hero-villain, for the characteristics of the poem's protagonist derive from *St. Irvyne's* Ginotti.

To relieve himself of the curse of eternal life, Ginotti

---

[11]Butter, p. 46.

relates to Wolfstein the story of how his burdensome fate
began:

> "From my earliest youth, before it was quenched by complete
> satiation, curiosity, and a desire of unveiling the latent mys-
> teries of nature, was the passion by which all the other emotions
> of my mind were intellectually organized. This desire first led
> me to cultivate, and with success, the various branches of
> learning which led to the gates of wisdom. . . . Love I cared not
> for."

But this generally praiseworthy endeavor to develop his
mental faculties separates him from the community of men:

> "I had lived, hitherto, completely for myself; I cared not for
> others; and, had the hand of fate swept from the list of the living
> every one of my youthful associates, I should have remained
> immoved and fearless. I had not a friend in the world; — I cared
> for nothing but self."[12]

In these passages, Shelley directs our attention to a virtue
and a vice that are inextricably united: the commendable
trait of deepening one's intellectual life is shadowed by a
concomitant urge to forgo love and human sympathy. The
possibility implied is that curiosity may usurp one's human-
ity and tempt him toward the realm of the inhuman or super-
natural — this, as Ginotti quickly discovers, first by denying
God and then, for the promise of eternal life, by giving
himself to the devil. Consequently, the real question be-
comes that of how far one's passions must go, no mattter
what the object, before he has sinned — either against hu-
manity or against God. Ginotti's choice alienates him from
the human and the divine, and the particular kind of limbo
that ensues from that choice is a self-imposed curse. His
quest and his curse become one, and the resulting torment on
earth foreshadows his eternal torment.

  Similar to the searches for forbidden knowledge under-

---

[12]*The Complete Works of Percy Bysshe Shelley*, ed. Roger Ingpen and Walter E.
Peck (New York, 1965), 5:180-81.

taken by Maturin's Melmoth and Godwin's St. Leon, Ginotti's search leaves us with ambivalent feelings about the Gothic hero-villain, but there is no question of ambiguous feelings since the moral order in these works insists that we condemn a character who goes too far. William Axton states that

> morally ambiguous characters were thought to evoke in the reader the contradictory play between the judgment offered by the rational understanding and that presented by intuitive sympathy, two fundamentally opposed modes of insight and assessment. . . . Because an intuitive grasp of character circumvents abstract analysis and achieves a subconscious realization of the totality of its object, it was held to be a morally superior instrument of judgment. At the same time, however, the very conflict in the moral estimates of these two differing faculties lends a piquant ambiguity to the relationship of reader and work which was highly prized because of the added emotional intensity it offered. In short, the divided nature of the Gothic hero-villain is itself a blueprint of the romantic temperament and an embodiment of romantic critical theory.[13]

The psychological complexities that Axton indicates, the light and dark sides of the hero-villain that force us to move back and forth between reason and intuition, are indeed central not only to an understanding of the Gothic novel but also to the meaning of *Alastor*. As we turn to the poem, the problem of ambiguity and ambivalence will be crucial to a just interpretation of the action and theme.

After his invocation to nature, "Mother of this Unfathomable world" (18), the narrator recounts the history of a young poet, the wandering seeker of "Knowledge and truth and virtue" (158). Like Ginotti, the Poet undergoes special experiences:

> By solemn vision, and bright silver dream,

---

[13]William F. Axton, in the introduction to Charles Robert Maturin's *Melmoth the Wanderer* (Lincoln, Neb., 1961), pp. xi-xii.

His infancy was nurtured. Every sight
And sound from the vast earth and ambient air,
Sent to his heart its choicest impulses.
The fountains of divine philosophy
Fled not his thirsting lips, and all of great,
Or good, or lovely, which the sacred past
In truth or fable consecrates, he felt
And knew. When early youth had passed, he left
His cold fireside and alienated home
To seek strange truths in undiscovered lands.

                                                          (67-77)

Besides accounting for the basic quest motif in the poem, the passage gives slight hints, in such terms as "cold fireside," "alienated," and "strange truths," of the psychological and intellectual predisposition of the Poet that will introduce the curse motif. Both Ginotti and the Poet begin their young manhood on the same commendable note: to enlarge the mind. All avenues of knowledge are open to them, and each character, as is typical of the Gothic hero-villain, quickly reaches the frontiers of normal human possibility. Beyond this point lies the temptation of the occult or the superhuman, a temptation that this type of figure cannot easily resist.

As the Poet ascends to a new level of search, he visits exotic areas in Asia Minor and Africa: "His wandering step / Obedient to high thoughts, has visited / The awful ruins of the days of old" (106-8). Here, through study and contemplation of the monuments, he begins to understand "The thrilling secrets of the birth of time" (128). His journey into self-discovery has led him from a childhood encounter with nature to an exposure to "divine philosophy" (71) and finally to the discovery of the occult. But as he draws closer to ancient, mystical, and primitive experience, he ignores any chance for the human love that is offered to him, and which, in the preface to the poem, Shelley sees as being of vital importance:

Among those who attempt to exist without human sympathy, the pure and tender-hearted perish through the intensity and passion of their search after its communities, when the vacancy of their spirit suddenly makes itself felt.

An example of this occurs when an Arab girl brings him food and cares for him, but he is oblivious to her signs of affection; and being timid and coldly rebuffed, the girl, "to her cold home / Wildered, and wan, and panting, she returned" (138-39).

This instance is not exactly the same kind of rejection of human sympathy that Ginotti practices, but it brings on a similar kind of curse. At this point in his quest, the Poet could have chosen human love and compassion, for he senses "the vacancy of their spirit." Instead he selects the path of the esoteric explorer that leads him through strange lands and, at last, to the "vale of Cashmire" (145). The journey takes him deeper into the self, but the subtle tone of self-indulgence that develops signals a flaw in the character of the idealistic poet-hero; he verges on the villainy of self-ishness. Both Ginotti and the Poet are egocentric insofar as they are willing to sacrifice their contact with humanity for the sake of their respective visions. We have already mentioned the comparatively simple moral framework behind Ginotti's world, and his search for eternal life is based on bizarre and obvious temptations that can result only in his destruction; but, in the complex psychological world of the Poet, the seductive qualities of the aesthetic or spiritual life will prove to be equally destructive. In both cases, these characters take the luxurious leap into the unknown that life does not willingly afford, and the consequences of these actions are disastrous.[14]

The next section of the poem (140-91) is crucial, for here the Poet experiences a dream-vision that drives him to his

----

[14]Many scholars have discussed Shelley's urge to escape from the harsh realities and dull routine of the world, much as the Poet in *Alastor* does, but they fail to see that Shelley himself is aware of the dangers and is more critical, finally, of flight from reality than is usually realized.

death. Shelley carefully sets the atmosphere for visionary knowledge. In the "vale of Cashmire,"

> ... far within
> Its loneliest dell, where odorous plants entwine
> Beneath the hollow rocks a natural bower,
> Beside a sparkling rivulet he stretched
> His languid limbs. A vision on his sleep
> There came, a dream of hopes that never yet
> Had flushed his cheek. He dreamed a veilèd maid
> Sate near him, talking in low solemn tones.
> Her voice was like the voice of his own soul
> Heard in the calm of thought. . . .
>
>   (145-54)

This inner meeting with the self — its deepest desires and wishes — engenders a trance, symbolized by sexual intercourse with the veilèd maid. Shortly we will return to the significance of the dream-vision and the exotic elements of nature surrounding the experience, but our interest now is in the subjective state, with its unique rewards and damning punishment, that the Poet enters. He will find that, just as Ginotti pays with his soul for the promise of eternal life on earth, so, too, the Poet's dream of fulfillment carries its own form of curse.

When the Poet awakens and finds the maid gone, we are told the meaning of the dream:

> The spirit of sweet human love has sent
> A vision to the sleep of him who spurned
> Her choicest gifts.
>
>   (203-5)

In other words, because the Poet, in his pursuit of the ideal, has ignored the demands of love that nature instills in each of us, his fate is to be visited by a sudden recognition of an intense and desirable love and then to discover that it has escaped him. At this juncture, the curse motif takes effect.

The Poet begins his wanderings again, not in quest of know-
ledge and delight with the world but in anxious toil to recap-
ture the creation of his own imagination. The psychological
condition that develops is similar to that which overtakes
Ginotti: the Poet and the hero-villain long for death because
life has become bitter and meaningless without love. Con-
fronted with existences thus rendered bleak, they consider
death as the only possible choice.[15]

It is easy to see why those critics and scholars who have
missed the curse motif in *Alastor* would call Shelley incon-
sistent and why to them the title *Alastor; or the Spirit of
Solitude* might seem forced. In the first place, they think the
author has complete sympathy for the Poet, whereas the
truth of the matter is that Shelley's response is
ambivalent—he both approves and disapproves of the young
idealist who would sacrifice all for a dream. In the second
place, they fail to recognize that "Solitude" is a curse, not a
blessing or an escape. Without knowing it, the Poet seeks the
very thing that destroys him. The "cold fireside" and
"alienated home," which were physical realities, have now
become mental realities, about which Shelley justly says,
"The Poet's self-centered seclusion was avenged by the
furies of an irresistible passion pursuing him to speedy
ruin." There is no confusion or inconsistency here; in fact, it

---

[15]Shelley and Thomas Medwin treat the same idea in a joint effort entitled *The
Wandering Jew* (1810). This long poem is a youthful and completely Gothic produc-
tion, but it bears further witness to Shelley's perennial interest in the curse motif
and in the suffering hero. Thus, the following passage is illustrative of the predica-
ment not only of the poem's central figure, Paulo, but also of that which confronts
Ginotti and the Poet in *Alastor*:
        "Rack'd by the tortures of the mind,
        How have I long'd to plunge beneath
        The mansions of repelling death!
        And strove that resting place to find
        Where earthly sorrows cease.
                                                (727-31)
The poem is not usually included in Shelley's works because Medwin claims credit
for most of it, but see the introduction to *The Wandering Jew*, ed. Bertram Dobell
(London, 1887) and also Shelley's letters nos. xi, xiv, xvi in *Complete Works 8*, for
evidence to the contrary.

is wholly logical, even necessary, as we shall see, that a person with the refined sensibilities possessed by the Poet should unwittingly convert his obsession into a curse. Loss of control over one's destiny, either through his own fault, as is the case with the Poet, or through the fault of fate, as happens to the Wandering Jew, results in irrevocable doom. Haunted by the memory of his vision—"At night the passion came, / Like the fierce fiend of a distempered dream" (224-25)—and unable to rediscover it, the Poet's wanderings must now point toward death. To understand properly this impulse to find his vision or destroy himself in the attempt, the reader must turn to the early section of the poem and analyze the sequence of visionary experience that leads to the Poet's curse.

In the invocation to nature, Shelley employs a mode that was very typical of his Gothic "votary of romance" period:

>   I have watched
> Thy shadow, and the darkness of thy steps,
> And my heart ever gazes on the depth
> Of thy deep mysteries. I have made my bed
> In charnels and on coffins, where black death
> Keeps record of the trophies won from thee,
> Hoping to still these obstinate questionings
> Of thee and thine, by forcing some lone ghost
> Thy messenger, to render up the tale
> Of what we are. In lone and silent hours,
> When night makes a weird sound of its own stillness,
> Like an inspired and desperate alchymist
> Staking his very life on some dark hope,
> Have I mixed awful talk and asking looks
> With my most innocent love. . . .
>
>   (20-34)

The narrator's attempt to plumb the meaning of life by questioning the significance of death, and the process described in this passage by which he seeks for meaning, lead us immediately to anticipate a world of superreality.

Graveyards, ghosts, and the occult are the external means he
finds suitable for the purpose of portraying his internal dis-
coveries. He has acquainted himself with nature and its two
extremities of life and death until, at last, his intuitions give
him partial insight, signaled by the word *enough*, into the
"deep mysteries" of life and into "the deep heart of man":

> . . . though ne'er yet
> Thou hast unveiled thy inmost sanctuary,
> Enough from incommunicable dream,
> And twilight phantasms, and deep noon-day thought,
> Has shone within me. . . .
> . . . .
> . . . that my strain
> May modulate with murmurs of the air,
> And motions of the forests and the sea,
> And voice of living beings, and woven hymns
> Of night and day, and the deep heart of man.
>
> (37-49)

Though it does not require extensive analysis, this first men-
tion of "incommunicable dream, / And twilight phantasms
and deep noon-day thought" can be taken as a suggestion
that dreams and visions are possible and perhaps the only
way to understand certain levels of existence. The passage is
primarily descriptive and a prelude to the method of vi-
sionary poetry, but it does establish the distinction between
the experience of the narrator, the poet in the invocation,
and the young idealistic Poet described throughout the rest
of the poem.[16] The two poets have similar but not identical
sensibilities—a crucial point that will help us determine the
poem's actual intention.

---

[16] As a general principle, this study will avoid, whenever possible, the practice of
referring to Shelley as the narrator or charcter in any given poem. Unfortunately,
much scholarly confusion has arisen when the author has been equated with the
figures in his works. Such has been the case not only in *Alastor* but also in such
works as "Ode to the West Wind," "Hymn to Intellectual Beauty," *Adonais*, and
other major poems.

Shelley's analytic mind orders the second dream-vision as a dramatization of the first and as an interlude and preparation for the third and most important visionary experience. No doubt Shelley is fully conscious and careful of the pattern he imposes, for the process by which the poetic (or creative) consciousness is developed, illumined, and then destroyed (because of the pursuit of impossible ideals) conforms to his carefully reasoned preface to the poem. When we consider the conditions that preceded the second vision—the visits to famous ruins of antiquity, the attentive study of ancient man's attempt to fathom the meaning of life—we are not surprised when the Poet's experience brings him to a point of hyper-consciousness:

> He lingered, poring on memorials
> Of the world's youth, through the long burning day
> Gazed on those speechless shapes, nor, when the moon
> Filled the mysterious halls with floating shades
> Suspended he that task, but ever gazed
> And gazed, till meaning on his vacant mind
> Flashed like strong inspiration, and he saw
> The thrilling secrets of the birth of time.
>
> (121-28)

This history resembles the visits to charnel houses: the ghosts and occult suggestions of the first vision have become the "speechless shapes" and "floating shades" of the second. The parallel can be extended so that the visionary experience that partially understands "the deep heart of man" compares to the insight into "the thrilling secrets of the birth of time." When we consider comparisons between the first and the second visionary instances, however, we should not hastily think that the experiences of the narrator are precisely those of the Poet-protagonist. At the end of the invocation and after the description of the narrator's dedication to nature and the exploration of her secrets, the narrator says, "I wait thy breath, Great Parent." He infers that because of his visionary experience he has come to a knowledge of "the deep heart of man" and that, through inspiration, he will now communicate it to others. Immediately following this promise, the narrative of the Poet begins, but after his first visionary experience we realize that he has no dedication similar to the one that the narrator made in the invocation; on the contrary, the hero is uninterested in communicating the "thrilling secrets" he has learned from his wanderings. Instead of seeking human contact, he pursues his self-centered way toward the third instance of dream-vision.

The disaster that grows out of the third visionary state returns us to the quest-curse motif and indicates how tightly knit the three visions are. The first two offered diverse choices, and the reader can determine how the narrator and the Poet reacted after their respective visions, but the third vision offers no choice, for the Poet has already, figuratively speaking, sold his soul to the devil, much as Ginotti had done.[17] By thus exploring the complex relationships in visionary experience, Shelley raises the quest-curse motif to a metaphysical level.

We have already seen how the third dream-vision begins as a meeting of the self with the soul, which Baker refers to as the "psyche-epipsyche" concept: "the mind (psyche) imaginatively creates or envisions what it does not have (epipsyche), and then seeks to possess epipsyche, to move towards it as a goal. Therefore the psyche-epipsyche strategy in a nutshell is the evolution by the mind of an ideal pattern towards which it then aspires."[18] As the dreaming Poet

---

[17]Recalling the main points raised about the dream-vision of the Gothic tradition, one can compare them with the third vision in *Alastor*: a highly emotional stage in the development of the dreamer, a supernatural figure or event, a dream that embodies a truth hidden from the dreamer in his waking hours, and finally the need to interpret and act upon the dream, which begins to haunt him.

[18]Baker, *Shelley's Major Poetry*, p. 53. The same concept is also applied to *The Revolt of Islam*, *Prometheus Unbound*, *Epipsychidion*, *Adonais*, and "The Triumph of Life."

creates this ideal pattern, concretized in the form of the
veilèd maid, he formulates an abstraction that might well
exist in one realm of experience but that completely fails to
materialize in another. To state the problem differently,
when we create our paradise in the sky, it is usually impossi-
ble to re-create it on earth. One should look more closely,
however, at the kind of reality that a dream-vision can be
before further pronouncements on the fate of the Poet are
made.

Besides "Knowledge and truth and virtue . . . / And lofty
hopes of divine liberty," the veilèd maid is said to represent
"poesy, / Herself a poet" (158-61). She is a strange combina-
tion of abstraction and sensuality, for as the Poet and the
maid silently commune, she slowly becomes an exciting
object of sexual desire:

>   . . . he turned,
> And saw by the warm light of their own life
> Her glowing limbs beneath the sinuous veil
> Of woven wind, her outspread arms now bare,
> Her dark locks floating in the breath of night,
> Her beamy bending eyes, her parted lips
> Outstretched, and pale, and quivering eagerly.
> His strong heart sunk and sickened with excess
> Of love.
>
> (174-82)

Obviously, the abstraction has become so intense that the
Poet's mind must form recognizable concrete symbols
within which an "ideal pattern" can be embodied. In a
dream-vision, one finds the freedom to transfer his myriad,
disjointed, and confused waking experience into a concen-
trated image, a pristine insight into a reality that the con-
scious mind is normally denied: as Shelley's preface states,
"the vision in which he embodies his own imaginations
unites all of wonderful, or wise, or beautiful, which the poet,
the philosopher, or the lover could depicture." But the vi-

sion contains an ambiguous edge by which the maid changes into a temptress figure who seeks to possess the Poet completely:

> He reared his shuddering limbs and quelled
> His gasping breath, and spread his arms to meet
> Her panting bosom: . . . she drew back a while,
> Then, yielding to the irresistible joy,
> With frantic gesture and short breathless cry
> Folded his frame in her dissolving arms.
> Now blackness veiled his dizzy eyes, and night
> Involved and swallowed up the vision; sleep,
> Like a dark flood suspended in its course,
> Rolled back its impulse on his vacant brain.
>
> (182-91)

From the line "Folded his frame . . ." and on to the conclusion of the poem, the Poet is no longer free. The definite signs of the curse motif have begun to accompany those of the quest. This psychic experience, with its various details, contains the ingredients of the Gothic dream-vision and of the first two visions in the poem, but now they are carried to their extreme: there is nothing—by definition—beyond the ideal, and what the Poet has known as real in his dream cannot be re-created as ideal in his waking life. Blinded by his obsession, the Poet fails to see the contradiction between his essential desires and his existential possibilities.

Thus, following the lines of the Gothic tradition, we see Shelley bringing the Poet to a highly refined and emotional peak in his development and then using the dream-vision to introduce a supernatural figure who will inform the dreamer of a truth central to his existence. The truth, as we have noted, is the Poet's search for an ideal image that symbolizes "all of wonderful, or wise, or beautiful," and which, for a moment, he believes is found in the form of the maid. Because of the nature of ideal truth, he could not conceptualize it while fully conscious, but the visionary state takes him beyond the common restrictions that waking experience imposes. Unfortunately for the Poet, the final condition, the interpretation of the dream, is the point where he makes his disastrous mistake, for the dream is true and yet deceptive at the same time.

Shelley develops a circumstance in which the Poet fails to interpret his dream correctly and "seeks in vain for a prototype of his conception." In effect, the idealistic Poet allows his dream to indicate a way of action finally destructive to him because it attempts too much. From this viewpoint, the dream can be read as a warning, which the poet is not wise enough to understand; the dream embodies the hero's deepest wishes, but seen properly, it also cautions us that such ideal fulfillment is unattainable. Though visionary experience may inform the Poet what he really wants and might pursue, life may not permit him to find it, for the vision that he has is so perfect, both spiritually and physically, that it cannot be found in life. This ambiguous situation determines the grounds for asserting the curse motif in the poem, and though the third dream-vision occurs early, its repercussions work throughout the lengthy history of the Poet's dissolution and justify Shelley's preface completely. For further understanding of Shelley's conception, one can continue along the lines of the quest-curse convention and its relationship to the Poet's mind and to nature, the "Great Parent" (45).

When the Poet awakens, the reader is struck by Shelley's use of external phenomena to mirror the condition of the Poet's mind.[19] "The imagery of *Alastor*. . . is used expressionistically to convey the physical, mental, and spiritual states of the Poet and his close relationship with his surroundings."[20] We shall see, however, that because of his alienation from other human beings, nature, in turn, cannot save her protégé, who becomes a victim of his "spirit of

---

[19]See Earl R. Wasserman's chapter on "Mont Blanc," in *The Subtler Language* (Baltimore, 1959) for one of the most extended treatments of Shelley's complex use of mental imagery. Aspects of Wasserman's method are relatable to *Alastor* and many of Shelley's other poems.

[20]Hildebrand, p. 50.

solitude,'' a kind of Gothic spirit.

The process by which Shelley delineates a drastic change in the Poet's psychology is seen through the mood and tone of the passage immediately following his experience with the veilèd maid:

> Roused by the shock he started from his trance—
> The cold white light of morning, the blue moon
> Low in the west, the clear and garish hills,
> The distinct valley and the vacant woods,
> Spread round him where he stood. Whither have fled
> The hues of heaven that canopied his bower
> Of yesternight? The sounds that soothed his sleep,
> The mystery and the majesty of Earth,
> The joy, the exultation? His wan eyes
> Gaze on the empty scene as vacantly
> As ocean's moon looks on the moon in heaven.
>   (192-202)

This stark scene of utter desolation reflects the abrupt transformation in the bond between the Poet and nature. Through such images as "cold white light," "the blue moon," "the clear and garish hills," and "the distinct valley and the vacant woods," Shelley delicately etches the lifeless world the Poet now faces. With the disappearance of his ideal, he is unable to respond to waking life, and the passage beautifully contrasts his past with his present and its foreshadowing of the future: the harsh, sharp sounds and images in the first five lines, which depict his present disarray, oppose the smooth music and scenery of the next four, which evoke his past, and the last two lines engender a full sense of the melancholy, so welcome to the Gothic spirit, that will accompany the Poet to his end. This opposition of mood and tone is an aid in developing the ambivalent response Shelley makes toward the Poet and his fate, and which is deftly captured in the final image of the reflecting moon and its mirrored counterpart in the sky. Shelley's treatment of this situation supports the argument that the dream-vision is ambiguous, that it is both an ideal and a curse, and that whatever happens to the Poet can be affirmed and condemned at the same time. The apparent contradiction here is precisely why so many scholars have mistakenly called Shelley inconsistent, and our attention must finally focus on this point. First, however, let us study the pattern of ambiguity that runs through the Poet's quest and Shelley's method of exposing the pattern.

As the journey to death begins, Shelley explicitly states the basis for the Poet's error:

> He eagerly pursues
> Beyond the realms of dream that fleeting shade;
> He overleaps the bounds.
>
> (205-7)

For him who would take one form of reality "beyond the realms of dream" and who, in so doing, "overleaps the bounds" that separate the visionary from the waking state, there is a dire risk of losing his place in the scheme of life, the "given" world, upon which he had formerly depended. The Poet finds that his obsession destroys his delight in nature and turns all he knows and sees into bitterness. Like the Wandering Jew, Wolfstein, and Ginotti, he becomes a seeker after death, for the peace he desires cannot be found on earth:

> The cottagers,
> Who ministered with human charity
> His human wants, beheld with wondering awe
> Their fleeting visitant. The mountaineer,
> Encountering on some dizzy precipice
> That spectral form, deemed that the Spirit of Wind
> With lightning eyes, and eager breath, and feet
> Disturbing not the drifted snow, had paused
> In its career. . . .
>
> (254-62)

In the process of rejecting nature and human companionship, he turns more and more into himself, and the spirit of solitude draws him further and more mercilessly toward psychological and physical suicide; he comes to resemble, in form and attitude, the haunted figure of the Gothic hero-villain. What we soon realize is that Shelley intends to depict the destruction of the Poet through a slow disintegration of his psychological and physical contact with the external world. The poem becomes a labyrinthine exploration of the Poet's mind or, by extension, of any mind that has had its ideal vision, has tried to recapture the vision in actual life (an impossibility), and, failing to do so, turns in upon itself and dies.

To accomplish the subtle task of picturing the dissolution of the Poet's mind, Shelley employs a number of techniques that, far from involving mere fantasy or ornamentation, are thematically and stylistically necessary to his purpose. In various ways and at various times, journey and quest, both on land and water, go deeper into the mental world; personification regularly shows the influence of nature, solitude, and the ideal on the Poet's consciousness; and the action is everywhere surrounded by profuse and exotic imagery that, not at all the exercise in "purple patches" that many critics have termed it, is logically suited to the entire temper of the death motif.[21] These general characteristics require specific examples to bring out their Gothic quality.

The journey through strange lands is an ambiguous venture of search and flight:

> Lost, lost, for ever lost,
> In the wide pathless desert of dim sleep,

---

[21]The following is a typical example of the failure to see the significance of the imagery in the latter part of the poem: "In *Alastor* the wanderings of an all-too-gentle poet furnish the occasion for extended descriptions, often sonorous and impressive though heavy with adjectives, in the course of which any 'meaning' that may have been intended is lost." R. D. Havens, "Shelley the Artist," in *The Major English Romantic Poets*, ed. Clarence D. Thorpe, Carlos Baker, and Bennett Weaver (Carbondale, Ill. 1957), p. 183.

That beautiful shape! Does the dark gate of death
Conduct to thy mysterious paradise,
O Sleep? Does the bright arch of rainbow clouds,
And pendent mountains seen in the calm lake,
Lead only to a black and watery depth,
While death's blue vault, with loathliest vapours hung,
Where every shade which the foul grave exhales
Hides its dead eye from the detested day,
Conducts, O Sleep, to thy delightful realms?
This doubt with sudden tide flowed on his heart,
The insatiate hope which it awakened, stung
His brain even like despair.

                                                        (209-22)

The tension between images of hope and Gothic images of
despair here and in the remainder of the poem encourages a
continual dialectical relationship between quest and escape
from the quest, between death and sleep that resembles
death, and finally between ecstatic communion with nature
and the dreadful loss of that communion. The pattern of
ambiguity is sustained from the third dream-vision to the
poem's conclusion; and this passage typifies the hesitation
and sympathy with which Shelley affirms the Poet on the one
hand and condemns him on the other. Though sympathetic,
Shelley indicates that the Poet's fault lies in the way he goes
about his quest—by cutting himself off from communion
with others, he destroys the very source of poetry itself:
language, which perforce has value only insofar as it links
men to their fellows. Furthermore, his solitary journey from
place to place becomes a form of dissipation that ensures
self-destruction, and his physical and spiritual isolation as-
sumes all the feverish marks of the Gothic quest—the same
quest that drives Wolfstein, Ginotti, St. Leon, and Melmoth
to their destructions.

Evidence of the Poet's error occurs when he is unable to
relate to the cottagers who give him food and lodgings
(254-71), and in the next stanza he compounds the error. He
compares himself to a beautiful swan that he disturbs on

"the lone Chorasmian shore" (272), and as the bird flies off,
the Poet says:

> "Thou hast a home,
> Beautiful bird; thou voyagest to thine home,
> Where thy sweet mate will twine her downy neck
> With thine, and welcome thy return with eyes
> Bright in the lustre of their own fond joy.
> And what am I that I should linger here,
> With voice far sweeter than thy dying notes,
> Spirit more vast than thine, frame more attuned
> To beauty, wasting these surpassing powers
> In the deaf air, to the blind earth, and heaven
> That echoes not my thoughts?"
>
> (280-90)

Ironically, the Poet is wasting his powers because of self-
deception, for he pities himself to the point where he is
incapacitated. Aware of his own possibilities, he denies their
fruition by trying to unite with a dream. His "desperate
hope" (291) is always accompanied by "a shadowy lure, /
With doubtful smile mocking its own strange charms"
(294-95). From this line on, the Poet's disturbed mind begins
to experience sights and sounds that neither he nor we can be
sure are "real":

> Startled by his own thoughts he looked around.
> There was no fair fiend near him, not a sight
> Or sound of awe but in his own deep mind.
>
> (296-98)

The argument that the Poet's journey has become as much
inward as it is outward[22] will be based on further examples of
hallucination that occur shortly, and it will be clear that the

---

[22]See Hildebrand, pp. 46-59, for a close, albeit tiresome, discussion of the Poet's
journey. Unfortunately, the literal approach that is applied, esp. pp. 56-59, abso-
lutely nullifies Shelley's poetic conception.

furies in his own mind— similar to the image of Victoria that haunted Wolfstein—create the strange, phantasmagorical world in which the Poet dies. As noted in the first chapter, the mind in a state of hallucination is important to the Gothic tradition because such a condition permits the uncertainty, the ambiguity of human experience to partake of the mysterious and the supernatural. To the Poet, death becomes the object of his search, for in its mystery he wonders if the world beyond might contain the ideal figure of his dream vision. Left with no other direction to pursue, he enters a small boat "to embark / And meet lone Death on the drear ocean's waste" (304-5). His complete physical and psychological dissolution distinctly remind us of the harried appearance of the Gothic hero-villain.

The whirlwind that drives the Poet's boat across the ocean to the cliffs of the Caucasus is another mental excursion — this time through terrible dangers—but the Poet remains entirely passive before the onslaught of wind and wave. He is numb to the forces of the external world until he thinks that the meaning of the voyage is clear:

> The boat fled on,—the boiling torrent drove,—
> The crags closed round with black and jagged arms,
> The shattered mountain overhung the sea,
> And faster still, beyond all human speed,
> Suspended on the sweep of the smooth wave,
> The little boat was driven. A cavern there
> Yawned, and amid its slant and winding depths
> Ingulfed the rushing sea. The boat fled on
> With unrelaxing speed.—"Vision and Love!"
> The Poet cried aloud, "I have beheld
> The path of thy departure. Sleep and death
> Shall not divide us long!"
>
> (358-69)

The reader sees that a major change in mood begins to take place. The Poet's helplessness is found in nature's control of his destiny. Before, he had relentlessly pursued his ideal, but as soon as he abandons himself to death, the "Great Parent" directs the external action of the poem.

The basic strategy that Shelley follows is common to the Gothic tradition; that is, imagery and particularly personification provide a direct emotional and intellectual contact so that we are able to attend the Poet through a weird wonderland, half mental and half physical. This strange landscape will contain spirits, visions, and a profusion of nature imagery directed toward specific ends. In the above passage, the boat is a vehicle to begin the transportation of the Poet's soul through initial tempestuous experience—the wild sea and the threatening cliffs—and, he thinks, lead him to his " 'Vision and Love!' "

Symbolically, nature does lead the Poet to his death, but it does not cause that death; the curse, the spirit of solitude, remains the self-imposed agent of destruction. The Poet's journey down into a cavern, along a mighty river, and to the brink of a huge whirlpool can plausibly be interpreted as one possible way to find death—a rapid and complete obliteration of consciousness. But one of nature's chance winds saves the boat and

> . . . with gentle motion, between banks
> Of mossy slope, and on a placid stream,
> Beneath a woven grove it sails, and, hark!
> The ghastly torrent mingles its far roar,
> With the breeze murmuring in the musical woods.
> Where the embowering trees recede, and leave
> A little space of green expanse, the cover
> Is closed by meeting banks, whose yellow flowers
> For ever gaze on their own drooping eyes,
> Reflected in the crystal calm.
>
> (399-408)

Thus the Poet is presented with a temporary reprieve, and we notice that the mood of nature has become one of calm and delight after the narrow escape from the "ghastly torrent.'' Presumably the mind turns from an immediate and dramatic encounter with death to a scene of beauty and peace. The scene, however, stands tinged with a melancholy that immediately recalls the overriding quest-curse motif of the Gothic mode:

> The wave
> Of the boat's motion marred their pensive task,
> Which nought but vagrant bird, or wanton wind,
> Or falling spear-grass, or their own decay
> Had e'er disturbed before. The Poet longed
> To deck with their bright hues his withered hair,
> But on his heart its solitude returned,
> And he forbore. Not the strong impulse hid
> In those flushed cheeks, bent eyes, and shadowy frame
> Had yet performed its ministry. . . .
>
> (408-17)

The allegory of the despairing mind being saved from the abyss, confronted with a moment of tranquillity, then tempted to partake of life's ''bright hues'' once again, finally returns to the curse of solitude and the quest for the ideal. Personification is managed with extreme delicacy here and in the following passage when the Poet leaves the boat and wanders through an exotic forest. His eye encounters the signs of life, harmony, and joy that nature offers, but his mind is passive to the hints that surround him. At this point a pervasive gloom, so congenial to the Gothic sensibility, overtakes the hero and becomes the poem's dominating mood.

A different mode of personification is used when the Poet approaches a dark well. He peers meditativly at his own reflection in the water, but at length becomes aware of a strange figure that materializes from nature's agents:

> A Spirit seemed
> To stand beside him—clothed in no bright robes
> Of shadowy silver or enshrining light.

Borrowed from aught the visible world affords
Of grace, or majesty, or mystery;—
But, undulating woods, and silent well,
And leaping rivulet, and evening gloom
Now deepening the dark shades, for speech assuming,
Held commune with him, as if he and it
Were all that was,— only . . . when his regard
Was raised by intense pensiveness . . . two eyes,
Two starry eyes, hung in the gloom of thought,
And seemed with their serene and azure smiles
To beckon him.
                                                              (479-92)

Shelley intensifies the power of nature on the Poet's mind so that the vague and various feelings he experiences combine to form the appearance of a spirit; personification, in this instance, moves beyond suggestion and into another example of "psyche-epipsyche" dimension, very similar to the dream-vision of the veilèd maid. This scene is the fourth example of visionary activity in *Alastor*, and it embodies again the same major characteristics that we discovered in the Gothic tradition. But in this particular case the vision is interrupted by "two starry eyes, hung in the gloom of thought"—the Poet's succubus, the ideal, challenges his communion with the "Great Parent." Certainly the passage is meant to indicate the original two possibilities still open to the Poet: he can find communion with nature and avoid death, or he can pursue his ideal into death. It is the latter choice that he makes. Nature can do no more now than simply accompany her favorite charge to his destruction, for her redemptive quality is ignored.

"Obedient to the light / That shone within his soul" (493-94), the Poet follows a stream that he equates with the complexity of his own psychological history.[23] The sur-

---

[23]One should compare Shelley's "Essay on Life" and "A Treatise on Morals" for a discussion of his thoughts, influenced by David Hume, on the relationship between the laws of the mind and the laws of the universe. See *Shelley's Prose*, ed. David Lee Clark (Albuquerque, N. M. , 1954), esp. pp. 174 and 182. Hereafter this source will be noted as *Prose*.

rounding landscape, obviously relective of the Poet's state
of mind, changes from an Arcadian setting to one of inferno-
like desolation; the Gothic atmosphere is omnipresent:

> Grey rocks did peep from the spare moss, and stemmed
> The struggling brook: tall spires of windlestrae
> Threw their thin shadows down the rugged slope,
> And nought but gnarled roots of ancient pines
> Branchless and blasted, clenched with grasping roots
> The unwilling soil. A gradual change was here,
> Yet ghastly.
>
> (527-33)

The adjectives "grey," "spare," "struggling," "thin,"
"gnarled," "ancient," "branchless and blasted," "grasp-
ing," and "unwilling" are external aspects of nature indica-
tive of the Poet's outer physical and inner mental condition.
Indeed, the lines immediately following the above section
explicitly draw a parallel between the Poet and the stark
world about him. We are reminded of the melancholic Wolf-
stein standing on the cliff or of similar scenes from Shelley's
juvenile "graveyard" poetry.[24] But the key word in such a
Dantesque underworld is *ghastly*. The total effect of this
particular stanza (514-70), in imagery, music, and thought, is
to indicate the barren end of the Poet's quest, his hopeless
ideal, and his wasted life. The sense of futility is complete,
and *ghastly* is not too strong a word to typify the imagery of
"black gulfs and yawning caves" (548), "the howl / The
thunder and the hiss of homeless streams" (565-66), and
"the pass expands / Its stony jaws" (550-51); nor can we
ignore the harsh, discordant sounds of "the abrupt mountain
breaks, / And seems, with its accumulated crags, / To over-
hang the world" (551-53) and "A pine, / Rock-rooted,
stretched athwart the vacancy" (561-62); finally come the

---

[24]Varma, pp. 197-99, presents a cursory but pertinent discussion of Gothic
characteristics in *Alastor* and in a few of Shelley's other poems.

terrible implications of the last few lines when the reader
compares them to the Poet's life:

> . . . whilst the broad river,
> Foaming and hurrying o'er its rugged path,
> Fell into that immeasurable void
> Scattering its waters to the passing winds.
>
> (567-70)

For in the previous stanza, the Poet had despairingly paral-
leled the mute forces of nature with the futility of his "living
thoughts" (512) when his "bloodless limbs shall waste / I'
the passing wind" (513-14).

The gloomiest thought in the poem is the idea of meaning-
lessness, of nothingness, that the Poet experiences and that
seems to tempt the narrator as he sadly meditates on the
vacancy caused by the disappearance of a "surpassing
Spirit" (714) whose qualities were beyond expression and
whose loss can only leave a feeling of "pale despair and cold
tranquillity" (718).[25] All the Poet's excellent potential has
withered and died because of an impossible quest, and
Shelley's grasp of the absurdity of the situation leaves us
with a haunted sense of the human mind's cruel deceptions,
for the Poet has tried to objectify a dream.

It is not accidental that the Poet finds "one silent nook"
(572) within the wasteland of the mind in which to die: the
spirit of solitude had finally "performed its ministry" (417),
now that nature was unable to help the Poet, now that the
ideal he had diligently pursued had deserted him, and now
that his own body and mind had wasted away. The extinction
of the Poet's consciousness is a natural consequence of the
action in the poem, for his mind had conceived of an ideal, he

---

[25]Shelley's sense of the possible absurdity and futility of life is very distinct and
appears in many of his major poems through terms like *vacancy*, *gulf*, *void*, *abysm*,
annihilation, *intense inane*, *senseless death*, etc. See James Rieger, *The Mutiny
Within* (New York, 1967), who speculates that Shelley, because of profound depres-
sion, may have attempted suicide at the time of his accidental drowning.

then sought it in an impossible journey (as much mental as physical), and finally, in despair, the mind relinquishes its hold on consciousness. His last sense impression is of the horned moon setting behind "the jaggèd hills" (649), before the quietness of death overtakes him:

> . . . the Poet's blood
> That ever beat in mystic sympathy
> With nature's ebb and flow, grew feebler still:
> And when two lessening points of light alone
> Gleamed through the darkness, the alternate gasp
> Of his faint respiration scarce did stir
> The stagnate night:—till the minutest ray
> Was quenched, the pulse yet lingered in his heart.
> It paused—it fluttered.
>
> (651-59)

Again, we are reminded that the tips of the horned moon, the "two lessening points of light," are the same force as the "two starry eyes," and the ideal of the veilèd maid haunts the Poet until the moon sets; only then does he die.

Shelley ends the poem on a eulogistic note. He laments that there is no "wondrous alchemy" (672) to bring the Poet back to life. Comparisons are then made to the elixir vitae and the Wandering Jew, which recall the Gothic figures of Ginotti and Wolfstein, but the Poet's fate cannot be changed, nor should it. Thus, ". . . let no tear / Be shed—not even in thought" (702-3), for the death of such a refined being as the Poet is beyond weeping.

Unfortunately, many scholars have simply taken the eulogy and that part of the preface to *Alastor* which aligns with it to signify that Shelley is in complete sympathy with the Poet. This inaccurate interpretation has served as the basis for taxing Shelley with inconsistency, since the preface also contains the remarks about "the furies of an irresistible passion." The doubts as to whether or not there is a curse motif in the poem are unfounded, and one should see that

quest and curse motifs are equally present, are not at all
contradictory, and, in fact, are indispensable to the expres-
sion of Shelley's complex thought:

> the poem and the Preface are complementary to each other.
> Shelley formulates in the latter ideas which receive proper
> poetic treatment in the former.[26]

Shelley is both sympathetic with the Poet's obviously noble
quest for the ideal and critical of it because of the curse of
solitude that the quest brings. His attitude, then, is ambiva-
lent, for the vision of the ideal becomes an ambiguous bles-
sing. And because of Shelley's viewpoint, we cannot agree
with scholars such as Carlos Baker, who states that

> the poem is an attempt to show, more or less symbolically, the
> intensity of one highly sensitive being's search for the "com-
> munities" of sympathy. The curse-motif is in the title and the
> preface alone. The erotic vision leading to a passionate quest
> was originally, and remained finally, the real central motif of
> Shelley's poem.[27]

This kind of statement is a failure to appreciate the intricacy
of Shelley's accomplishment and to see that this allegory "of
one of the most interesting situations of the human mind" is,
in terms of the conflict between the real and the ideal,
psychologically true and eloquently states a permanent di-
lemma that the idealist faces.

Throughout this chapter, my view has been that a more
precise understanding of the poem is assured if one relates
the poem and its preface to those conventions from the
Gothic tradition with which Shelley was wholly familiar: the
hero-villain, the quest-curse, the dream-vision, atmospheric
imagery, and personification. Constantly refining these fea-
tures, Shelley uses them artfully to discharge the difficult

---

[26]Gérard, p. 176.

[27]Baker, *Shelley's Major Poetry*, p. 47.

task of bringing the reader to see and to feel the melancholy beauty of a poet defeated by a passion seemingly beyond reproach. If we consider the tenderness with which Shelley observes the Poet, but also the destiny the Poet chooses, it is clear that Shelley can neither completely approve nor completely disapprove of the ideal and its blind pursuer, and in this ambivalence he is justified. For his hero-villain is exactly that: hero, but not completely so, and thus destined to a quiet, desperate death; villain, but embarked on an undertaking nobly inspired, and so worthy of our understanding and sympathy.

3

The Use of Gothic Elements
in the Mature Poetry

Although no other poem in Shelley's mature work follows the Gothic tradition so directly as *Alastor* does, individual poems do contain frequent echoes of the earlier work and prove a continuing allegiance to Gothic conventions and an indication of a persisting Gothic sensibility. In conjunction with this allegiance, these poems also provide an insight into Shelley's intellectual, philosophic, and aesthetic development.[1] Thus, when examining a number of poems from the period 1816-22, my intention is not to analyze the complete operation of Gothic elements in particular poems, which would become an unwieldy and unnecessarily repetitious task, in form if not in content; rather, the purpose of this chapter is solely to illustrate the presence of Gothic elements and through such demonstration to prove how

---

[1] This study can not concern itself with arguing for or against any particular aesthetic or philosophic approach to Shelley. He has been termed by diverse scholars and critics as an eighteenth-century rationalist and materialist, a political and social radical, a compromiser, a coherent but unsystematic thinker, the only true poet of Platonism, a Christian, an atheist, and a sceptic. Of course, all of these positions can be found in his work; they merely attest to the complexity of his mind and remind us that working with Shelley does not allow for simplistic categorization. See Carlos Baker, *Shelley's Major Poetry* (Princeton, 1948), pp. 273-74 for a succinct summary of the poet's intellectual development.

essential they were to Shelley's interests. Furthermore, I will again depend on the Gothic preoccupation with the hero-villain figure associated with the journey or quest-curse, the dream-vision that menaces or haunts its victim, terrifying imagery and personification, and such secondary issues as sex, the demonic, and the occult to substantiate my claim. It will quickly become apparent that in some poems Gothic elements are many and obvious, whereas in others these elements are used sparingly and do not herald a more complex and refined use of the tradition. In fact, because Shelley refines his art as he refines his experience, Gothic trappings will be virtually lost at certain points, and one will have only the appearance of a Gothic sensibility before him. Nonetheless, examination of the poems leads one to agree with Benjamin Kurtz when he states that "Shelley rarely gave up an idea or an emotion. The history of his mind and of his art is the continual repetition, with ever deeper realization and more entranced utterance, of ideas, moods, and patterns that are discernible very early in his work."[2] And what we can anticipate is Shelley's gradual and often subtle blending of Gothic conventions with personal, social, political, aesthetic, and philosophic interests as his poetic powers increase. In order more clearly and succinctly to align Gothic conventions with Shelley's major interests in the later poetry, it will be helpful now to establish the general characteristics of the Gothic tradition that recur in poems following *Alastor*.

After its usage in *Alastor*, the Gothic hero-villain convention first indicated in *Zastrozzi* and in *St. Irvyne* changes variously. Sometimes the protagonist is unqualifiedly heroic and completely affirmed in Shelley's eyes; at other times we are confronted with essentially villainous figures; but more often than not, Shelley portrays someone whose psychology represents an abstract state, someone whose motives and

---

[2]Benjamin P. Kurtz, *The Pursuit of Death* (London, 1933), p. 8.

actions are extremely complex and ambiguous.[3] The obvious external and melodramatic characteristics that surrounded Zastrozzi, Verezzi, Matilda, Ginotti, Wolfstein, and Megalena have, in the mature work, usually become intellectual and moral symbols designed to parallel the intricate processes of the mind. The inquiry in the previous chapter provides a fortunate structure for viewing the modifications Shelley deemed necessary for his loftier aims, and the demonstration in this chapter will attempt to show the dimension that he ultimately attains in using the idea of the hero-villain as an archetype for profound psychic experience. In many instances, we will once more see that Shelley is presenting, as he did in *Alastor*, a kind of allegory of the human mind, and that allegory can be made clearer by recognizing it as part of the Gothic mode.

The hero-villain and his quest-curse situation were emphasized in *Alastor* for two principal reasons: first, because the seeker of experience, knowledge, or the ideal is central to the Gothic romance tradition,[4] and second, because his quest-curse situation serves a narrative and dramatic function necessary to an understanding of the poem. Modifications of the situation occur frequently in the mature poetry and always in such a way that they determine the direction and meaning of the poem. Thus, when I refer to the Gothic hero-villain figure and the quest-curse convention in the poems that follow, I mean that the figure and his situation insure a specific Gothic atmosphere. Briefly described, this atmosphere derives from the external appearance of the

---

[3]See Peter Butter, *Shelley's Idols of the Cave* (Edinburgh, 1954), pp. 88-89 for an acute statement on Shelley's deep psychological insight into human motivation.

[4]One should, perhaps, include death as a major objective in the search and distinguish it from general experience. Aside from Ginotti and the Poet in *Alastor*, some of the more famous Gothic seekers after these goals are Radcliffe's Schedoni, Godwin's St. Leon, Maturin's Melmoth, Byron's Manfred and Cain, Mary Shelley's Frankenstein, and Goethe's Faust. For a brief description of the modern Gothic seeker and his quest, see Chester E. Eisinger, "The Gothic Spirit in the Forties," in *Pastoral and Romance*, ed. Eleanor Terry Lincoln (Englewood Cliffs, N. J., 1969), pp. 289-96.

hero-villain, matched by a distinct moral pose; his quest carries a curse, and though beginning as outward experiences, they normally turn inward; his search is for some kind of peace, of respite, or for meaning in life; his psychological state is one of uncertainty and melancholy; he stands as an isolated figure who challenges the accepted order of things, sometimes on a purely worldly level but more often than not on a spiritual plane; his experience generally encompasses metaphysical personages and mysterious forces of nature; and finally, his Gothic quest demands a charged atmosphere that permits the awesome in human physical and psychic reality.

Though virtually all of the characteristics just mentioned appear, albeit crudely, in Shelley's early work, the most dramatic and significant discovery one makes in most of the mature work is the process by which Shelley begins his poem with a more or less conventional Gothic hero-villain but then artfully converts him into a romantic hero.[5] When one recalls the normally destructive tendency in the Gothic tradition and opposes that impulse with Shelley's mature commitment to affirm, to idealize human experience, it becomes clear why this process is so crucial to an understanding of many later poems. On a more general level, one scholar interprets this practice as follows:

> Gothic and romantic writing spring alike from a recognition of the insufficiency of reason or religious faith to explain and make comprehensible the complexities of life. We may distinguish between Gothic and romantic in terms of what they do within this situation. The imagination, Coleridge tells us, reveals its presence "in the balance or reconciliation of opposite or discordant qualities." Romantic writing reconciles the discordant elements it faces, resolving their apparent contradictions imaginatively in the creation of a higher order. Gothic writing . . . has no such answers and can only leave the "opposites" con-

---

[5] In those poems where this process does not apply—especially in "The Triumph of Life" and in *The Cenci*—the persistent theme is one of chaos and destruction, to both physical and psychological powers.

tradictory and paradoxical. In its highest forms romantic writ-
ing claims the existence of higher answers where Gothic can
find only unresolvable moral and emotional ambiguity.[6]

Recognizing Shelley's strong desire to resolve life's con-
tradictions helps account for the virtual disappearance of
Gothic elements at particular points in the development of
many mature poems, and this fact should leave us with no
discomfort that there are definite limitations on the extent to
which the Gothic tradition can be applied to Shelley's work.

Like the hero-villain convention, the Gothic dream-vision
feature also has a restricted application in this chapter. Cer-
tainly, there are few instances where Shelley does not use
the visionary mode in the later poetry, but unless dream-
visions serve as a type of experience that intimidates and
threatens to destroy, they can hardly be considered as
Gothic. What will be particularly useful, I believe, is the
method whereby the Gothic dream-vision sets off other
forms of visionary experience and enhances their role. Most
critics have, regrettably, ignored the different kinds of
dream-visions that present themselves in Shelley's poetry,
and thus one often reads comments that view his visionary
practice as a flight from reality, a commitment to a Platonic
world of forms, obscuratinism for its own sake, or an indica-
tion of repressed sexual aberrations.[7] It is not the task of this
study to respond to these positions, except indirectly, but I
do wish to argue, as I did in the study of *Alastor*, that
Shelley's visionary poetry can be understood best as a plaus-
ible and significant means of suggesting different levels of
reality. Furthermore, my study continues to treat the

---

[6]Robert D. Hume, "Gothic Versus Romantic: A Revalution of the Gothic
Novel," *PMLA* 84 (1969): 289.

[7]In one way or another, the following works read Shelley's dream-visions from
these points of view: Eustace Chesser, *Shelley & Zastrozzi: self-revelation of a
neurotic* (London, 1965); J. A. Notopoulos, *The Platonism of Shelley* (Durham, N.
C., 1949); James Rieger, *The Mutiny Within* (New York, 1967); and Edward
Carpenter and George Barnefield, *The Psychology of the Poet Shelley* (London,
1925).

dream-vision as a "practical" instrument for portraying and analyzing extremely involved states of consciousness that accommodate, as in *Alastor*, intellectual, sexual or emotional, and spiritual awareness.

Refining this awareness is partially accomplished through a refinement in Shelley's use of the Gothic dream-vision. This need for a more sophisticated approach in the use of visionary experience is noted by Glenn O'Malley when he refers to synesthesia in *Queen Mab*:

> But if Ianthe is synesthetic, Shelley must soon have recognized that his expression of her visionary powers was too crudely and confusingly supernatural. What he required to develop this aspect of his vision theme was to make his synesthetic agent or medium not a disembodied spirit, but a person whose refinement of perception, while possibly approaching the supranormal, remained essentially human.[8]

Indeed, the Gothic dream-visions we will see are all of a type that can be based on possible human experience, and such creations as ghosts, demons, or other supernatural figures disappear or become projections of the imagination, with the single exception of *Prometheus Unbound*. One easily concurs with F. L. Jones when he says that Shelley's use of the visionary mode is remarkable because "no other single theme contains so much of Shelley's conception of himself, of his basic philosophy of love, beauty, and truth, and of his spiritual life"[9]; but my emphasis must be on the type of visionary performance that includes the personal suffering that precedes the idealized states just mentioned. In this sense, the Gothic dream-vision is a purgative device, a warning that the victim must interpret correctly so that he can

---

[8]Glenn O'Malley, *Shelley and Synesthesia* (Evanston, Ill., 1964), p. 42. This work provides a lengthy account of Shelley's use of synesthetic imagery, which the author defines as that "language which describes one sense experience in terms that 'belong' to one or more of the other senses" (p. 3).

[9]F. L. Jones, "The Vision Theme in Shelley's *Alastor* and Related Works," *SP* 64 (1947): p. 125.

arrive at a more perfect state of existence, for if he fails to understand the dream-vision, his destruction will follow. In Shelley's mature poetry, it will become apparent that the menacing characteristics of the Gothic dream-vision feature that appeared in *Zastrozzi, St. Irvyne*, the early poetry, and *Alastor* have been converted into instances of major and abiding poetic value.

A final area to consider before illustrating this assertion is that of imagery and personification. In *Alastor*, we saw how Shelley employed imagery, especially that from nature, and personification to capture the relationship between the mind and the external world. Again, it is impractical to apply the lengthy kind of analysis that was used in *Alastor*, not only because of methodological repetition but also because other studies of Shelley's imagery anticipate the procedure, if not the exact material, that one would use.[10] Instead, my plan is to include a brief statement about the value of Gothic imagery in some of the major poems that will be reviewed and then examine one mature poem closely to appreciate the precise operation of Gothic imagery in relation to the poet's intention. The principle of selection will be modest and restrict itself to those images and figures that are related to the Gothic tradition or that partake of circumstances we can term Gothic.

The "Ode to the West Wind" (1819) is the particular poem that will serve as a central example of Gothic imagery and personification, but since discussion of the poem will come late in this chapter, it is advantageous to recall and expand upon Shelley's use of imagery now for the sake of the poems that come before the "Ode." For this discussion *Alastor* again aids us because the history of the Poet indicated how imagery and personification became a part of that poem's

---

[10]Particularly see R. H. Fogle, *The Imagery of Keats and Shelley* (Hamden, Conn., 1962); Glenn O'Malley; Oscar Firkins, *Power and Elusiveness in Shelley* (Minneapolis, Minn., 1937); Rieger (*The Mutiny Within* is excellent for tracing the sources of some of Shelley's Gothic imagery); and Leone Vivante, *English Poetry* (Carbondale, Ill., 1963), pp. 127-82.

allegory: when the narrator appeals to the muse, nature ("Great Parent"), a mythological universe is created and peopled with ghosts, phantasms, a veilèd maid, forms, spirits, and strange shapes, all of which assume certain human characteristics. Through the personification of these abstractions, Shelley indeed formulated an allegory of the human mind, and it became apparent how the careful use of imagery acts to fulfill an internal as well as external function.[11] Moreover, it was argued that imagery often directs the action in a poem and constructs an imaginative world that we can legitimately accept without offense to our rational faculties: one's experience may assure him that there are no spirits or demons in the world, but his imagination convinces him that they can be created from his uncertainties, fears, and hopes. Shelley would intuitively agree with Jung's statement that

> primitive man impresses us so strongly with his subjectivity that we should really have guessed long ago that myths refer to something psychic. His knowledge of nature is essentially the language and outer dress of an unconscious psychic process. But the very fact that this process is unconscious gives us the reason why man has thought of everything except the psyche in his attempts to explain myths. He simply didn't know that the psyche contains all the images that have ever given rise to myths, and that our unconscious is an acting and suffering subject with an inner drama which primitive man rediscovers, by means of analogy, in the processes of nature both great and small.[12]

Because nature imagery and personification have a psychic

---

[11]I am indebted to a discussion with Professor Schulze for the development of the outline stated here. Mythopoeia is integral to an analysis of Shelley's imagery, but such a large topic goes beyond the limits of this study, which does not and cannot claim to offer a complete explanation of the function of personification. I will restrict myself to the role of Gothic qualities in the conception of pesonified elements. See Harold Bloom, *Shelley's Mythmaking* (New Haven, 1959), esp. chapter I for extensive definition of mythopoeia in Shelley's poetry.

[12]*The Basic Writings of C. G. Jung*, ed. Violet Staub de Laszlo (New York, 1959), p. 290.

counterpart, then, their importance can be stressed as indices to the Gothic mode.

"Good imagery," Fogle notes, "is richly evocative, various in the implications of its meaning. It is complex, broad of scope. Other things being equal, the best imagery will give us the most ideas, the most complex relationships, the widest span of experience."[13] And in *Alastor*, as in most of the later poetry, much of the imagery grows directly out of Shelley's early involvement with the Gothic romance. One should not be surprised, therefore, at Shelley's recurrent use of turbulent images to depict states of mind agitated by hate, fear, grief, or other intense passions and then oppose those conditions with extraordinarily tranquil and sublime images, for the poet seeks to reveal the "complex relationships" that exist between the dark and light forces within us. Since Shelley's imagery has, in the main, a distinct didactic or thematic intention behind it, my argument insists that Gothic imagery is utilized, ultimately, to accentuate the idealistic content Shelley seeks to present.

Turning to Shelley's major poems, we confront the immediate problem of organizing a number of examples to suit a logical pattern that indicates the poet's Gothic sensibility and the use to which he puts it. My approach to the problem attempts to be as straightforward as possible: first, a few examples will be presented in which Gothic elements predominate; second, a group of poems that embody aspects of the Gothic tradition to serve particular ends will be used; and third, a small body of poems will help us see the process whereby Gothic elements disappear in the major poetry. Illustration and succinct analysis, the central concern for the remainder of this chapter, should establish the necessary pattern of thought and lessen the need for lengthy summary of plot and theme in the poems.

---

[13]Fogle, p. 24.

I

One finds in a fragmentary poem like "Prince Athanase" (1817) characteristics of the hero-villain convention and a curse-quest dilemma similar to that which caused the demise of the Poet in *Alastor*:

> There was a youth, who as with toil and travel,
> Had grown quite weak and gray before his time;
> Nor any could the restless griefs unravel
>
> Which burned within him, withering up his prime
> And goading him, like fiends, from land to land.
>
> (1-5)

The poem's more than three hundred lines convince us that the Prince's quest for ideal love is modeled on *Alastor*, and his haunted apperance warns the reader that his fate is likely to be as dire as that of the Poet's. The resemblance between the two young men remains incomplete, however, for there develops a difference of mood in the poems that causes one to view the Gothic sensibility from another perspective. First, the effects of the curse differ: the Prince's curse becomes more subtle and oppressive than the Poet's because Athanase is deeply afflicted by melancholy and world-weariness throughout the poem—a psychological malaise that finds its Gothic predecessor in Wolfstein and Verezzi rather than in Ginotti and Zastrozzi. This condition produces introspection and moodiness in the Prince and a meditative air in the poem that, except for the narrator's invocation and the final scenes, is generally absent in the more frenzied action of *Alastor*. The introspective air surrounding the Prince informs us that his quest is internal (very little action takes place) and seems to intensify his curse, his "restless griefs." In turn, a self-awareness and quiet, mysterious acceptance of approaching death permeates his thoughts and reveals a mental complexity that was lacking in the Poet of

Alastor. Shelley's intention appears to be that of using the Gothic mode to focus our attention on states of melancholy and psychic dissolution arising from forces that have no direct referent in the external world; the Prince's Gothic quest is almost wholly internal, and the mood of mystery is furthered by expressionistic descriptions of his suffering:

> For like an eyeless nightmare grief did sit
>
> Upon his being; a snake which fold by fold
> Pressed out the life of life, a clinging fiend
> Which clenched him if he stirred with deadlier hold;—
> And so his grief remained—let it remain—untold.
>
> (120-24)

and

> . . . but o'er the visage wan
> Of Athanase, a ruffling atmosphere
>
> Of dark emotion, a swift shadow, ran,
> Like wind upon some forest-bosomed lake,
> Glassy and dark.
>
> (210-14)

This imagery does not explain or clarify the prince's condition but, rather, serves to accentuate the dark state of his mind and also to draw the reader into the inscrutable Gothic mood of the poem. Here and in the next few poems, the impulse behind the poetic conception drives relentlessly toward defeat and death (though in the following example the death of the hero and heroine are portrayed as a victory of the spirit), and Shelley's general inclination is to leave us with unanswered questions and feelings of doubt and ambiguity.

"Prince Athanase" and *Alastor* deal mostly with the isolated individual consciousness and its personal Gothic quest, but it is also worthwhile to observe how Gothic elements can be employed to further social and political beliefs. The two poems most suitable for my purposes are *The Revolt of Islam* and *Hellas*, for they depend strongly upon Gothic conventions to develop both action and theme.

Written in the wake of the frustrated hopes of the French Revolution, *The Revolt of Islam* (1817) is Shelley's lengthiest poetic interpretation of religious, political, and social tyranny and of the means to overcome them so that man can live in freedom, equality, and love.[14] To execute this lofty intention, the complicated narrative of the poem centers on the activities of Laon and Cythna, whose history includes many elements from the Gothic tradition: the young, intense seeker of knowledge and experience accompanied by a lover who braves all dangers with him, a semi-incestuous union (in the original version of the poem she is his blood sister, but Shelley's publisher insisted that the relationship be altered because of the ensuing incest theme),[15] the master-slave situation, abductions and imprisonments, terror, melancholy, and innumerable occult or supernatural occurrences that depend on nature imagery and the dream-vision for their presentation. One must restrict the poem's rich Gothic possibilities to a few adventures of the hero and heroine, however, for I wish to emphasize only those characteristics that advance the argument in a specific direction.

---

[14]In the preface to the poem, Shelley describes his didactic aim: "I have sought to enlist the harmony of metrical language, the ethereal combinations of the fancy, the rapid and subtle transitions of human passion, all those elements which essentially compose a Poem, in the cause of a liberal and comprehensive morality; and in the view of kindling within the bosoms of my readers a virtuous enthusiasm for those doctrines of liberty and justice, that faith and hope in something good, which neither violence nor misrepresentation nor prejudice can ever totally extinguish among mankind." *Shelley's Prose*, ed. David Lee Clark (Albuquerque, N. M. , 1954), p. 315.

[15]See Montague Summers, *The Gothic Quest* (London, 1938), pp. 391-92 for the importance of the incest theme in Gothic literature.

Laon's history[16] begins in much the same way as that of the protagonists in *Alastor* and "Prince Athanase":

> I wandered through the wrecks of days departed
> Far by the desolated shore. . . .
> . . . .
> Around me, broken tombs and columns riven
> Looked vast in twilight, and the sorrowing gale
> Waked in those ruins gray its everlasting wail!
> (748-56)

From his journeys and musings Laon wakens to the terrible tyranny hanging like a pall over the people, and he vows, through a bloodless revolution, to overthrow the King. Cythna, an adopted sister, accompanies him in the attempt to arouse the populace, and one can argue that the usual concept of the hero-villain figure begins to divide, in this poem of immense proportions, so that the heroic efforts of the young couple are opposed by the villainous activity of the established order; an important Gothic image is merely converted, not lost, as idealism struggles against brutal reality.

The introduction of the female counterpart to Laon (she is sometimes called Laone and reminds one of a Jungian anima figure) receives great attention and her character is developed as fully and carefully as his. Very apparent is the fact that she represents the theme of female emancipation and is an equal partner in man's striving to free himself from the bonds of custom, outmoded and irrationally conceived and administered institutions, and physical and psychologi-

---

[16]Two articles, Walter Graham's "Shelley and *The Empire of the Nairs*," *PMLA* 40 (1925):881-91 and Kenneth Neil Cameron's "A Major Source of *The Revolt of Islam*," *PMLA* 56 (1941):175-206, are important studies for the background of the poem. The first article relates James Lawrence's novel, which Shelley knew well, and *The Revolt of Islam* to the "exotic Gothic" tradition that stems from Beckford's *Vathek*, but Cameron's study relates Shelley's poem to the "social Gothic" mode and sees C. F. C. Volney's *Les Ruines* as the main source.

cal slavery.[17] Though she is portrayed as a heroine, her strength of character and determination to fulfill her destiny pattern themselves on some of the women who appear in Shelley's novels and in novels he had read: Matilda, Megalena, and Victoria (Dacre's *Zofloya*), to mention a few, resemble Cythna in will power and passion, and Eloise, Julia, and Antonia (Lewis's *The Monk*) reflect her modesty and compassion.[18] She becomes the perfect mate with whom Laon can unite his physical, intellectual, and spiritual energies. Inasmuch as Shelley devotes almost equal space to the individual adventures of Laon and Cythna, we begin to see that the author's true revolutionist combines the aspirations of male and female, of head and heart, and of flesh and spirit; the revolution they seek must free all members of society, including the tyrannical king, the priests, and other conventional symbols of oppression.

Throughout the adventures of the young hero and heroine runs a constant stream of violence, terror, and gloom; such events as the cruel separation of the lovers by the king's forces, the rape of Cythna by the king, the enchainment and torture of Laon (a close parallel in all essential details to the history of Verezzi), their respective seizures of madness and eventual escapes from the prisons that hold them, the temporary success of the revolution, its failure, and finally the execution of the revolutionary pair by fire are the elements of a plot that unfolds in an atmosphere of grotesqueness and morbidity. For example, a frenzied dream that comes to

---

[17] Crane Brinton writes, "Shelley expects a great deal from the aid of woman. Cythna is indispensable to Laon in his great work of reformation. And Cythna is the new woman, or rather, the natural woman, to whom the divine impulses of love necessary to the regeneration of the world have been given in a purer form than to man. Woman at present is a hindrance to man in his struggle for liberty, for she is bound by stronger chains of convention than he. But once she is free, she becomes the most precious of allies." *The Political Ideas of the English Romanticists* (Ann Arbor, 1966), p. 173.

[18] Cythna combines the energies of both the spirited and the virtuous woman of the Gothic tradition to become the sort of "precious" ally referred to by Brinton. She also embodies characteristics that, in Prometheus's Asia, appear in subdued form and, in Beatrice Cenci, are reversed, as will be indicated in the next chaper.

Laon exemplifies the physical revulsion and spiritual horror embodied in much of the poem:

> A woman's shape, now lank and cold and blue,
>   The dwelling of the many-coloured worm,
> Hung there; the white and hollow cheek I drew
>   To my dry lips—what radiance did inform
>   Those horny eyes? whose was that withered form?
> Alas, alas! it seemed that Cythna's ghost
>   Laughed in those looks, and that the flesh was warm
> Within my teeth!—A whirlwind keen as frost
> Then in its sinking gulfs my sickening spirit tossed.[19]
>   (1333-41)

This passage is fairly representative of the many images of worms, charnel houses, corpses, fiends, and other forms of horror that develop from scenes of panic, carnage, plague, and death.

Interestingly, these many Gothic accents alternate with passages of an extremely lyrical and idealistic nature that almost always grow out of the sexual attraction existing between Laon and Cythna. For Shelley, sexual love is simply another way of uniting physical, intellectual, and spiritual faculties, and his early interest in sex and free love, apparent from his Gothic novels and poetry, has persisted into his mature poems. One recalls the complex love situations in *Zastrozzi* and *St. Irvyne* and remembers Shelley's use of sex as an integral component of the novels' thought and action for the purpose of exposing intense physical and psychic energies: Verezzi and Matilda, Wolfstein and Megalena, and Ginotti-Nempere and Eloise follow a conventional Gothic pattern whereby illicit love leads to destruction, but, at the same time, Shelley advocates a belief in free

---

[19]Cf. the story of Cythna's abduction and Laon's gruesome dream with "Zeinab and Kathema," one of Shelley's juvenile poems, for similarities in characterization, plot, and setting. *The Esdaile Notebook*, ed. Kenneth Neil Cameron (New York, 1964), pp. 148-54.

love.[20] In his novels, it is apparent that sex and free love are used as much to shock and thrill the reader as they are to state an intellectual conviction, but the higher thematic objectives in *The Revolt of Islam* force an alteration in the Gothic pattern. Whereas earlier, sex became a wild, unfettered way of introducing great crimes of the flesh and the spirit, in the case of Laon and Cythna it is a means, through compete union, to escape the immediate threat of destruction: in the later poetry love is a regenerative impulse that orders physical and mental activity, not destroys it. An example of this alteration occurs after Laon and Cythna have escaped the king's forces and are hiding in an ancient Gothic-like ruin. The revolution they led has been defeated, and as they turn to one another for comfort, cosmic and natural agents combine with human desire and despair to mark the only salvation to which they have recourse — namely, love:

>   . . . and through a rent
> Of the ruin where we sate, from the morass,
>   A wandering Meteor by some wild wind sent,
>   Hung high in the green dome, to which it lent
> A faint and pallid lustre; while the song
>   Of blasts, in which its blue hair quivering bent,
> Strewed strangest sounds the moving leaves among;
> A wondrous light, the sound as of a spirit's tongue.

>   The Meteor showed the leaves on which we sate,
>   And Cythna's glowing arms, and the thick ties
> Of her soft hair, which bent with gathered weight
>   My neck near hers, her dark and deepening eyes,
>   Which, as twin phantoms of one star that lies
> O'er a dim well, move, though the star reposes,

---

[20]In the "Notes on Queen Mab" (1813), free love is viewed as more worthy than marriage because "love withers under constraint: its very essence is liberty: it is compatible neither with obedience, jealousy, nor fear: it is there most pure, perfect, and unlimited, where its votaries live in confidence, equality, and unreserve." *Prose*, p. 115.

Swam in our mute and liquid ecstasies,
Her marble brow, and eager lips, like roses,
With their own fragrance pale, which Spring but half
    uncloses.

The Meteor to its far morass returned:
    The beating of our veins one interval
Made still; and then I felt the blood that burned
    Within her frame, mingle with mine, and fall
    Around my heart like fire; and over all
A mist was spread, the sickness of a deep
    And speechless swoon of joy, as might befall
Two disunited spirits when they leap
In union from this earth's obscure and fading sleep.
                                                    (2615-40)

The wholly sensuous imagery here reminds one of the passage in *Alastor* where the Poet and the veilèd maid unite, and both poems derive their character types, physical setting, and form of sexual passion from Shelley's Gothic novels.[21] On a personal level, however, Laon and Cythna are able to escape the fragmentation and dissolution that afflict their Gothic ancestors, and the concluding section of the poem, after the young couple has been martyred at the stake, shows how the victims' spirits rise up out of disaster and are transported off to "The Temple of the Spirit." This alternation of accent between defeat on a worldly level and victory on a spiritual one is still in keeping with the Gothic tradition and less strange when understood as necessary to the development of the poem's major social and philosophic themes.

---

[21]Shelley describes, in "A Discourse on the Manners of the Ancient Greeks Relative to the Subject of Love" (1818), his mature view of love and sex: "the gratification of the senses is no longer all that is sought in sexual connection. It soon becomes a very small part of that profound and complicated sentiment which we call love, which is rather the universal thirst for a communion not merely of the senses but of our whole nature, intellectual, imaginative, and sensitive, and which, when individualized, becomes an imperious necessity, only to be satisfied by the complete or partial, actual or supposed fulfilment of its claims." *Prose*, p. 220. This attitude toward love is present not only in *the Revolt of Islam* but also in *Epipsychidion* and, in even more rarefied form, in *Prometheus Unbound*.

As one might expect from such an idealistic enterprise, the revolution fails because of the chicanery of the king and the priests and also because the people are not psychologically mature enough for freedom. Shelley spends a good deal of the poem elaborating on the peculiar attitudes that bind master and slave to one another, and the main point, repeated time and again, is how the same vicious cycle of slavery infects both King Othman and his subjects:

> For they all pined in bondage; body and soul,
>   Tyrant and slave, victim and torturer, bent
> Before one Power, to which supreme control
>   Over their will by their own weakness lent,
>   Made all its many names omnipotent;
> All symbols of things evil, all divine;
>   And hymns of blood or mockery, which rent
> The air from all its fanes, did intertwine
> Imposture's impious toils round each discordant shrine.
>   (730-38)

The "one Power" is symbolized in the poem as an eagle, the principle of evil, of hate and fear, and the Manichean universe envisioned in the work is deeply reflective of the Gothic world in which good and evil forces contend for the soul of man, a soul constantly harassed by the acute struggle between the light and the dark in man's experience. In his essay "On the Devil and Devils" (1819?), Shelley writes:

> The Manichean philosophy respecting the origin and government of the world, if not true, is at least an hypothesis conformable to the experience of actual facts. To suppose that the world was created and is superintended by two spirits of a balanced power and opposite dispositions is simply a personification of the struggle which we experience within ourselves, and which we perceive in the operations of external things as they affect us, between good and evil.[22]

---

[22]*Prose*, p. 265.

Laon and Cythna, of course, represent the principle of good, of love and trust, symbolized in the figure of the serpent. Releasing man from the curse of hate and slavery is their task, and though they are defeated and executed, their unfulfilled promise, as the earlier quotation from the preface to the poem states, survives in the people's minds.

It is probably not speculating too widely to see the Gothic hero-villain convention in *The Revolt of Islam* as the particularized image of a Manichean cosmos: on the one side stand Laon and Cythna and the occult forces of good that they represent, and on the other exist the forces of Othman and his powerful sources of evil. As seekers and promulgators of enlightenment, the hero and heroine are constantly opposed by the villain of ignorance, fear, and superstitition. The parallel can be extended so that good is the true and full union of diverse selves, while evil is dissension and antagonism among members of a society; the hero demands freedom, while the villain insists on repression; Laon and Cythna aspire to the ideal condition of the human spirit, while Othman works to degrade and humiliate humanity. Along this line of thought, the Gothic hero-villain becomes a microcosm for a Manichean universe and his dimensions expand to assume the philosophic assumptions of a specific world view. Though *The Revolt of Islam* abounds in Gothic attributes that derive from Shelley's earlier work, the poem offers him a new and unusual way to use the hero-villain for social and political intentions at a time in Europe's history when to be indifferent to such issues was, for Shelley, to be immoral.[23]

In *Hellas* (1821), one finds the theme of political oppression repeated, but the hero-villain feature assumes unprecedented, sophisticated characteristics not found in any other mature poem. Appearing once more is the figure of

---

[23]See Ronald Duerksen, *Shelleyan Ideas in Victorian Literature* (The Hague, 1966), pp. 14-18, for a cursory discussion of Shelley's concept of reformation and "ideal anarchism." Also included is his influence on Marx and socialism.

Ahasuerus, the Wandering Jew.[24] The hunted, fearful creature of *Queen Mab* has, however, nine years later become a self-possessed, noble creation of great magnitude and heroic proportions who quietly and prophetically reveals the folly, perennial rather than particular, of mankind. Opposing Ahasuerus, who proclaims the absolute value of the ideal and of the human spirit's freedom, one finds the villain and tyrant Mahmud—a much more complex character than the Gothic stereotypes of despicable monarchs and oppressors presented in *Queen Mab* and in *The Revolt of Islam*. Between these two agents, Shelley constructs a dialectic that reaches beyond the already noted master-slave cycle and raises the issue of the absurdity of human accomplishments.

Early in the play Mahmud wakes from a disturbing dream and says, as much to himself as to his confidant, Hassan,

> "Thrice has a gloomy vision hunted me
> As thus from sleep into the troubled day;
> It shakes me as the tempest shakes the sea,
> Leaving no figure upon memory's glass.
> Would that—no matter. Thou didst say thou knewest
> A Jew, whose spirit is a chronicle
> Of strange and secret and forgotten things.
> I bade thee summon him:—'tis said his tribe
> Dream, and are wise interpreters of dreams."
>
> (128-36)

Immediately, the dramatic interest centers on Mahmud, the significance of his dream, and the figure of the mysterious Jew so that peripheral issues like the battles between the Turks and the Greeks, the victories and defeats on both sides, assume minor proportions. Shelley's intention is one of indicating through Mahmud and the Jew that all conquest

---

[24]Rieger's *The Mutiny Within*, pp. 51-73, analyzes Shelley's interest in the Wandering Jew tradition and relates it to such diverse figures as Beatrice Cenci, Prometheus, and Jesus.

is a pyrrhic victory; that the quest to master the world and other people carries the curse, once more, of confounding the ideal and the real:

> ". . . this Whole
> Of suns, and worlds, and men, and beasts, and flowers,
> With all the silent or tempestuous workings
> By which they have been, are, or cease to be,
> Is but a vision;—all that it inherits
> Are motes of a sick eye, bubbles and dreams. . . . "
>
> (776-81)

In this passage, Ahasuerus informs Mahmud that his melancholy and his distempered, haunting dream are products of a confusion, an inability to see the illusory character of his activities.

So far, these descendants of conventional Gothic fiction, the villain's cruel quest, and the menacing dream-vision have all been carefully refined to raise the poem's abstract considerations beyond the usual level of the Gothic sensibility. Only by so doing can Shelley develop his major theme: instead of chasing dreams of victory and mastery over men, Mahmud is told,

> ". . . look on that which cannot change—the One,
> The unborn and the undying."
>
> (768-69)

For until he does, his life can be filled only with " 'Mutinous passions, and conflicting fears' " (884). The crux of the drama bears this message out on a universal scale: as long as man continues his drive to subjugate others and in so doing frustrate "the cause of civilisation and social improvement" (preface), he will be the pawn of a vicious pattern of bitter defeats and hollow victories, and his mind, victim of an illusion, will spawn confusion out of which will grow ever more confusion.

The Gothic way to destruction and death in this lyrical drama evolves out of the metaphysical confusion noted by Ahasuerus, for such chaos is translated into a ghastly reality that occurs in a vision representing one of the play's battles:

> "The sound
> As of the assault of an imperial city,
> The hiss of inextinguishable fire,
> The roar of giant cannon; the earthquaking
> Fall of vast bastions and precipitous towers,
> The shock of crags shot from strange enginery,
> The clash of wheels, and clang of armèd hoofs,
> And crash of brazen mail as of the wreck
> Of adamantine mountains—the mad blast
> Of trumpets, and the neigh of raging steeds,
> The shrieks of women whose thrill jars the blood,
> And one sweet laugh, most horrible to hear,
> As of a joyous infant waked and playing
> With its dead mother's breast, and now more loud
> The mingled battle-cry. . . . "
>
> (814-28)

In image and tone, these violent energies recall the terrible passions of the Gothic mode; it is the spirit, the temper, behind such passages that illustrates my thesis. Further evolution can be seen by focusing on the villain figure. What one remarks in a character like Mahmud is his great change from a typical Shelleyan oppressor into an introspective, doubting leader who has become cynical and disillusioned with his role in a world of meaningless strife. When the phantom of Mahomet appears and interprets the scene just quoted, Mahmud gains self-knowledge and a wisdom that permits him to see how the present and the future will only lead to the same folly as that practiced in the past; thus, when the news of success in battle is heard, the tyrant laconically exits with, " 'Victory! poor slaves!' " (930)—meaning, of course, slaves to illusion. Through the prophetic utterances of Ahasuerus and the phantom of Mahomet, whom the Jew

conjures up, Mahmud gains his insight into the futility of
striving for the victories tyrants normally prize.

And when Mahmud's teacher, the other half of the hero-
villain figure, is described, the sense of wonder, of eternal-
ity, that envelops him recalls to us the world of Gothic
mystery in Shelley's early work:

> "The Jew of whom I spake is old,—so old
> He seems to have outlived a world's decay;
> . . . .
> . . . but from his eye looks forth
> A life of unconsumèd thought which pierces
> The Present, and the Past, and the To-come.
> Some say that this is he whom the great prophet
> Jesus, the son of Joseph, for his mockery,
> Mocked with the curse of immortality.
> Some feign that he is Enoch: others dream
> He was pre-adamite and has survived
> Cycles of generation and of ruin."
>
> (137-54)

Here, the legend of the Wandering Jew becomes much more
than the straightforward device for attacking the concept of
God that Shelley used in *Queen Mab*. Previously, Ahasuerus
exposed God as a tyrant because of his eternal vengeance,
but now the Jew appears as a symbol of "the One," an
interpreter of the difference between appearance and reality.
He rises above his former rebellious nature, his hunted and
haunted earthly existence, and attains a Buddha-like grace:
"The serene wisdom which Ahasuerus acquired along with
his triumphant spirit finally became all-important, and he
last appeared as Thought itself."[25]

By expanding the mythical qualities of the legend, Shelley
builds up the suspense surrounding the Jew—" 'he dwells in
a sea-cavern /'Mid the Demonesi, less accessible / Than thou

[25]Grace Calvert Collins, "Shelley's Treatment of the Legend of the Wandering
Jew," Master's thesis, The University of North Carolina, 1961, p. 49.

Mahmud or God!' '' (163-65)—and endows him with occult, oracular powers that establish an objectivity to his proclamations. He becomes an archetype for the nonsubjective, beyond-time-and-space narrator who is very characteristic of and important to Shelley's poetry. Appearing out of strange circumstances, this figure of the old seer and mentor—a type of eternal mediator between the particular and the general—reveals and interprets truth for those who are bound up in time and space. He is the standard of ideal reality against which man's thoughts and actions are to be measured.[26] For our purposes, however, the most important point to be made about the Wandering Jew figure in *Hellas* must be that his effect is entirely psychological rather than supernatural: it is not simply Shelley's ''. . . deep and true interest in the occult''[27] that intrigues us, but his ability to refine a Gothic convention so that psychological truth can be revealed. The incident of Ginotti's frightening confrontation with the devil in *St. Irvyne* fades in significance beside the rich psychological influence of the Ahasuerus figure developed near the end of Shelley's career.

The last poem to be examined in which Gothic elements predominate is ''The Triumph of Life'' (1822). Though a fragmentary poem and though the final one he wrote, Shelley nonetheless depends on the Gothic tradition to develop the theme of the loss of one's ideals and the havoc that results from this loss. The hero-villain convention, for example, is subtly molded to form the figure of the Dantesque young narrator and that of the Virgilian Rousseau who leads him into deeper levels of consciousness. Of these two, my em-

---

[26]In various guises, the idea of the old seer or ''eternal timekeeper'' appears as Ginotti, the Fairy Queen in *Queen Mab*, Zonoras in ''Prince Athanase,'' the Hermit in *The Revolt of Islam*, Demogorgon in *Prometheus Unbound*, Rousseau in ''The Triumph of Life,'' and as minor figures in a few other poems. For biographical interest in this topic, see A. M. D. Hughes, *The Nascent Mind of Shelley* (Oxford, 1947) pp. 26-29; Newman Ivey White, *Shelley* (New York, 1940), 1: 47-48; and Mrs. Shelley's ''Note on *The Revolt of Islam*,'' in *The Complete Poetical Works of Percy Bysshe Shelley*, ed. Thomas Hutchinson (London, 1943), pp. 156-57.

[27]Carl Grabo, *The Magic Plant*. (Chapel Hill, N. C., 1939), p. 16.

phasis must be on Rousseau, for his external appearance —
" 'an old root which grew / To strange distortion out of the
hill side' " (182-83), his seerlike pose, his quest to find the
meaning of life, his curse that results from the inability to
find this meaning and yet become captive to the quest, his
melancholy, uncertainty, and isolation in combination with
his mysterious, awesome experiences are all related to the
Gothic mode. Rousseau's story is one of Shelley's best and
most complex presentations of the dark and evil side of life,
how it comes to exist, and the high price paid by those who
lose their ideals because they fail to " 'know themselves!' "
(212) The tragedy Shelley wishes to indicate goes beyond
that seen on a personal level in *Alastor* and equally beyond
the social and political level of *The Revolt of Islam*. In "The
Triumph of Life," the central tragedy is existence itself and
the human propensity to confound its ideal possibilities.

Shelley introduces the Gothic context in the poem through
the use of a dream-vision that takes place in the mind of the
young narrator. In his visionary state, he experiences the
sensation of intense consciousness and suddenly becomes
aware of a gruesome pageant passing before him:

Old age and youth, manhood and infancy,

Mixed in one mighty torrent did appear,
Some flying from the thing they feared, and some
Seeking the object of another's fear;

And others, as with steps towards the tomb,
Pored on the trodden worms that crawled beneath,
And others mournfully within the gloom

Of their own shadow walked, and called it death;
And some fled from it as it were a ghost,
Half fainting in the affliction of vain breath. . . .

(52-61)

The impression of total disarray, of frenzied fear, that

courses through this passage sets the tone for the remainder of the poem. In seeking an explanation for the chaos he witnesses, the narrator chances upon Rousseau, a member of this wild crew, who describes the meaning of the masquelike scene by aligning it with his own experiences and his quest to find the answer to the question "What is Life?"

In all essential respects, Rousseau's early history resembles that of the other young seekers discussed above. Born with high ideals and a pristine vision of life, he falls victim to a temptress, " ' A Shape all light' " (352), who leads him into corruption and finally toward the "mighty torrent" of which he is now a part.[28] At this point it is necessary to confess that Rousseau's Gothic quest becomes very rarefied indeed—not in form but in content—and one proceeds with the full realization that he is not speaking directly to the point of the Gothic; nonetheless, the following discussion is relevant to Shelley's complete works, especially in terms of the implications found in "The Triumph of Life," *Prometheus Unbound*, and *The Cenci*.

Rousseau tells the young narrrator:

> "Before thy memory,

> "I feared, loved, hated, suffered, did and died,
> And if the spark with which Heaven lit my spirit
> Had been with purer nutriment supplied,

> "Corruption would not now thus much inherit
> Of what was once Rousseau. . . . "
>
> (199-204)

----

[28]Scholars have proposed many divergent interpretations of "The Triumph of Life," and two important Shelley scholars are diametrically opposed as to the meaning of the "Shape" Rousseau meets. Baker, *Shelley's Major Poetry*, pp. 264-68, argues that she is a benevolent figure, while Bloom, *Shelley's Mythmaking*, pp. 265-72, sees her as evil. I agree with Bloom on this critical point, not only because he supports my thesis but also because his argument is more reliable in obtaining an overall judgment on the poem's meaning.

Since he has partaken fully of humanity's common experiences and now follows the ''Car of Life,'' attention is directed to the cause of his wretchedness and how his youthful promise went amiss. Before relating his particular story, however, he points out different important figures among the throng who also became slaves to the car: Napoleon, Voltaire, Frederick, Paul, Catherine, Leopold, Plato, Aristotle, Alexander, and unnamed dignitaries of church and state; only a few of history's outstanding personages, like Socrates and Christ, are missing. Thus, whatever afflicts Rousseau will also be that which destroys the best or greatest of mankind.

After the occult description of his birth (308-35) and his youth spent near nature (335-48), the ''Shape'' appears and offers him a liquid to drink that will presumably answer the questions ''whence I came, and where I am, and why—'' (398), but he does not have time to finish his questions before he takes the cup of nepenthe. After that a new vision appears—the ''Car of Life''—and the quest for the meaning of life is the beginning of Rousseau's curse.[29]

If one sees the ''Shape'' as an ambiguous, seductive figure who performs much the same function as the veilèd maid in *Alastor*, then Rousseau's error is, like that of the Poet, the confounding of the real and the ideal. The cup of nepenthe, of forgetfulness, causes him to lose his youthful creative vision, and instead of withstanding life's forces, as Socrates and Christ did, Rousseau confesses:

>   ''I among the multitude
> Was swept—me, sweetest flowers delayed not long;
> Me, not the shadow nor the solitude;
>
> ''Me, not that falling streams Lethean song;

---

[29]There are multiple visionary instances in the poem, and it is clear that Shelley is using them to take us further and further into human consciousness. From the original dream-vision of the narrator we are led deeper into the frightful, menacing Gothic dream-visions of Rousseau's subconscious.

Me, not the phantom of that early Form
Which moved upon its motion—but among

"The thickest billows of that living storm
I plunged, and bared my bosom to the clime
Of that cold light, whose airs too soon deform."

                                        (460-68)

The context of Rousseau's remarks indicates the process whereby the hero-villain deforms himself. Some failing, some misdirected step, leads him to attempt more than what his ideals, or in this case, life, will permit. Rousseau's suggestion that almost all of us are victims of the "Shape," that few escape the "Car of Life," leaves the reader in a kind of limbo. How is it that we are born with creative vision, with the ideal, and then lose it? What twist in our nature causes us to confuse our ideals and become trapped in a quest-curse syndrome?

Earlier, Rousseau identifies many great figures in the passing throng, and his explanation for their attachment to the "Car of Life" is

                    ". . . their lore

"Taught them not this, to know themselves; their might
Could not repress the mystery [mutiny[30]] within,
And for the morn of truth they feigned, deep night

"Caught them ere evening."

                                        (211-15)

Some lines later (300-304), he explains to the young narrator that he knows how he (Rousseau) fell victim to life and its

---

[30]The newest edition of Shelley's poems indicates that "mystery" should actually read "mutiny." Since I have been using the 1960 printing of the poems throughout the study, both the original and the newest reading of this word are included here. For example, see Rieger's *The Mutiny Within* for a variant reading.

car, but he cannot tell why. Ironically enough, the passage just quoted exactly fits Rousseau's idealized history in the poem, and, apparently, one must know himself well enough not to confuse his pristine vision, his imaginative powers — that which for Shelley was more real than anything else —with life's illusory, meretricious offerings. "The mutiny within," then, is the urge, the quest, on the part of every man to answer the questions, " 'whence I came, and where I am, and why.' " But when one turns to life itself for a response, as Rousseau did, rather than to his original ideal visions, a curse afflicts him.

In discussing "The Triumph of Life," I have tried to reverse my normal procedure of identifying Gothic elements that contribute a context for understanding Shelley's themes; instead, prime attention was directed to the conflict between the ideal and the real, for herein lies, one can argue, Shelley's most terrifying Gothic vision. If the collapse of the human spirit and its ideals is the meaning of his final poem, if all but a few men are doomed to follow the "Car of Life," then, for Shelley, the most destructive forces are not those that attack the body but those that conquer the spirit. The truest and most complete form of destruction in the Gothic mode becomes a spiritual one: the loss of human integrity, of human ideals, and as we proceed, *Prometheus Unbound* and *The Cenci* will, respectively, dramatize the psychological process whereby one escapes from "The Triumph of Life" or falls victim to it.

Before these major poems are analyzed, we will benefit from observing Gothic elements at work in a few other poems that are helpful in directing the thrust of the argument. The function of these elements will receive only brief description, but such an overview should forcefully complement the structure of Shelley's thought.

II

Besides skillfully tracing the development of Gothic literature and its assorted conventions, Railo's *The Haunted Castle*[31] formulates an interesting general comparison between the Gothic castle and the haunted mind of Gothic enthusiasts. He proposes that the labyrinths and secret passages of the medieval pile are reflective of the mind's inner workings. If we apply this proposition to "Mont Blanc" (1817) and its setting, it is not inappropriate to consider, from the narrator's viewpoint, the mountain and its ravine as a tremendous castle that mirrors the mind's uncertainties and wonderings:

> Dizzy Ravine! and when I gaze on thee
> I seem as in a trance sublime and strange
> To muse on my own separate fantasy,
> My own, my human mind, which passively
> Now renders and receives fast influencings,
> Holding an unremitting interchange
> With the clear universe of things around;
> One legion of wild thoughts, whose wandering wings
> Now float above thy darkness, and now rest
> Where that or thou art no unbidden guest,
> In the still cave of the witch Poesy,
> Seeking among the shadows that pass by
> Ghosts of all things that are, some shade of thee,
> Some phantom, some faint image; till the breast
> From which they fled recalls them, thou art there!
>   (34-48)

As the narrator's imagination, "in the still cave of the witch Poesy," pursues its "ghosts" and "some phantom" among the desolate scene so "rude, bare, and high, / Ghastly, and scarred, and riven" (70-71), it forms sense impressions into a pattern that represents a state of mind where the eternality of the mountain and its power become mental propositions — man learns from nature because he imposes order on

---

[31]Eino Railo, *The Haunted Castle* (New York, 1964). See pp. 276-79 for his discussion of Shelley's Gothic sensibility.

chaos.[32] At the conclusion of the poem, the narrator poses a question to himself and to the mountain:

> The secret Strength of things
> Which governs thought, and to the infinite dome
> Of Heaven is as a law, inhabits thee!
> And what were thou, and earth, and stars, and sea,
> If to the human mind's imaginings
> Silence and solitude were vacancy?
>
> (139-44)

The logic of the poem demands the answer that "the secret Strength of things" only exists because of the "mind's imaginings," because of the imagination's ability to unite subject and object. The narrator's "trance" thus gives him license to delve into the mysteries of the mountain, of the universe, and of his own mind, and to realize that they are one; in other words, "of what lies beyond the phenomenal world we can have absolutely no idea, for there is no idea that could have any other source than the phenomenal world."[33] In a poem like "Mont Blanc," Shelley's intellectual quest does use Gothic imagery and a mood of mystery and wonderment as he confronts the phenomenal world, but our greatest interest in this world derives from what it says about the mind.[34]

---

[32] Schulze qualfies this by stating that "the meaning of the universe is essentially a human meaning, even though the universe exists apart from the mind, and manifests a power to which man is subject." p. 90.

[33] Jung, p. 98.

[34] An interesting prose statement from Shelley's "A Treatise on Morals" (1812-1815?) can be compared to the phenomenological principle in "Mont Blanc": "thought can with difficulty visit the intricate and winding chambers which it inhabits. It is like a river whose rapid and perpetual stream flows outwards—like one in dread who speeds through the recesses of some haunted pile and dares not look behind. The caverns of the mind are obscure and shadowy; or pervaded with a lustre, beautifully bright indeed, but shining not beyond their portals. . . .

"Most of the errors of philosophers have arisen from considering the human being in a point of view too detailed and circumscribed. He is not a moral and an intellectual—but also and pre-eminently an imaginative being. His own mind is his law; his own mind is all things to him. If we would arrive at any knowledge which should be serviceable from the practical conclusions to which it leads, we ought to consider the mind of man and the universe as the great whole on which to exercise our speculations." *Prose*, p. 186.

The Gothic background in the "Hymn to Intellectual Beauty" (1816) appears noticeably in story, imagery, and personification. In particular, the fifth stanza of the "Hymn" seems to recapitulate, through terms, images, and an atmosphere faithful to the Gothic tradition, the events in *Alastor* prior to the Poet's dissolution:

> While yet a boy I sought for ghosts, and sped
>> Through many a listening chamber, cave and ruin,
>> And starlight wood, with fearful steps pursuing
> Hopes of high talk with the departed dead.
> I called on poisonous names with which our youth is fed;
>> I was not heard—I saw them not—
>> When musing deeply on the lot
> Of life, at that sweet time when winds are wooing
>> All vital things that wake to bring
>> News of birds and blossoming,—
>> Sudden, thy shadow fell on me;
> I shrieked, and clasped my hands in ecstasy!
>
> (49-60)

This passage states the quest motif, the emotional involvement, the reverie that brings on visionary experience, the appearance of a supernatural agent (imaginative or actual), and the ecstasy when one's object of desire is suddenly realized. Out of these considerations can be drawn many parallels to the story of *Alastor*, but because of deeper consciousness on the part of the "Hymn's" narrator than that possessed by the Poet, the poems end very differently. In the "Hymn" the narrator's dedication to describe the "awful shadow" (1) of the "Spirit of Beauty" (13) that haunts him and to remain steadfast in his devotion to it bespeaks an intention that purports more than the narrow gratification of self: whereas the Poet in *Alastor* searched for his vision externally and mistook the nature of the ideal, the narrator in the "Hymn" recognizes that the ideal is an internal reality whose greatest lesson is to teach one "to fear himself, and

love all human kind'' (84). The Gothic element of "fear" is
crucial here, for the dimensions of the self are expanded
through an awareness of the "dark reality" (48) that exists
on both sides of the grave: the disciple of intellectual beauty
must master his inner weaknesses, escape the "dark slav-
ery" (70) of the world (selfhood), in order to "love all human
kind.''

"The Sensitive Plant" (1820) also tries to dramatize the
relationship between the poetic imagination and the concept
of intellectual beauty. When the beautiful lady, the spirit of
love and beauty, dies, the creative vision symbolized by the
plant can no longer flourish and Shelley records its pending
decay in solemn Gothic tones:

> . . . the Sensitive Plant
> Felt the sound of the funeral chant,
> And the steps of the bearers, heavy and slow,
> And the sobs of the mourners, deep and low;
>
> The weary sound and the heavy breath,
> And the silent motions of passing death,
> And the smell, cold, oppressive, and dank,
> Sent through the pores of the coffin-plank. . . .
>   (III. 5-12)

But the quiet, melancholic air that ensues when intellectual
beauty fades undergoes a drastic change as time's effect on
the garden is depicted in images like "the head and the skin
of a dying man" (29), "the decaying dead" (64), "a leprous
scum" (66), "like a wolf that had smelt a dead child out"
(107), "rose like the dead from their ruined charnels" (113),
and countless other images of horror and destruction.[35] Ob-

---

[35] In Mario Praz's *The Romantic Agony* (London, 1933), much of the space that is
devoted to Shelley's Gothic sensibility centers on a comparison of *The Cenci* and
"The Sensitive Plant." See pp. 114-16.

viously, the intensity of the Gothic atmosphere in "The Sensitive Plant" increases as the disastrous consequences of the absence of intellectual beauty is felt. Then, at the conclusion of the poem, when the creative vision is near its lowest ebb and verging on extinction, Shelley reverses the psychological direction of the mood and rises out of his dark pattern and into a world of the one and the many: he insures his theme by opposing the Gothic and the ideal.

An even more ghastly vision than that portrayed in "The Sensitive Plant" can be recognized in Shelley's short poem "On the Medusa of Leonardo Da Vinci" (1819), which Praz quotes in entirety on the opening page of *The Romantic Agony*. Wholly unrelieved by any subdued or overt idealism, the sublime element in this poem informs us that Shelley has indeed captured the difference between the "beautifully horrid" and the "horribly beautiful":

> It lieth, gazing on the midnight sky,
>   Upon the cloudy mountain-peak supine;
> Below, far lands are seen tremblingly;
>   Its horror and its beauty are divine.
> Upon its lips and eyelids seems to lie
>   Loveliness like a shadow, from which shine,
> Fiery and lurid, struggling underneath,
> The agonies of anguish and of death.
>
> (1-8)

This "tempestuous loveliness of terror" (33) is no figure to frighten us in the conventional fashion usually attempted by the Gothic; instead, the concentrated horror engendered by the Medusa image is designed to attract and engulf us so that our customary resistance to evil fades: we accept completely the implications of pain and destruction because they are mysteriously beautiful and very appealing to dark impulses within us, impulses that thrill to such an image as

A woman's countenance, with serpent-locks
Gazing in death on Heaven from those wet rocks.
                                                    (39-40)[36]

In a poem like the "Medusa," then, the psychological impli-
cations are terrifying because they are so attractive, but the
sublime and its potential urge toward annihilation can be
converted into affirmative directions, as the "Ode to the
West Wind" (1819) will prove.

The choice of working with this ode is based on the follow-
ing considerations: first, the poem offers numerous exam-
ples of Gothic imagery that suit the poem's thematic de-
mands; second, the imagery is typical and found in other
major poems of Shelley; third, the ode is short and the
imagery can be studied so that the logical connections within
the poem are readily established; and last, the major theme is
central to Shelley's works and one that has not been fully
stressed before. Though the "West Wind" is not a Gothic
poem, we are again in the presence of a work where the
Gothic sensibility is at play, and our interest is in individual
images and how these images serve the overall visionary
position assumed by the poem's narrator.

He introduces the ode with "O wild West Wind" (1). This
invocation to the muse, an uncontrollable agent, is similar to
the plea seen in *Alastor* and in the "Hymn to Intellectual
Beauty," where the poet-narrators seek inspiration from
mythological sources that inhabit the world of the mind. The
poet continues,

. . . thou breath of Autumn's being,
Thou, from whose unseen presence the leaves dead

---

[36]It is true that the "Medusa" is not a major poem in the Shelley canon, but the
central image is related to the "veilèd maid" in *Alastor*, the "Shape" in "The
Triumph of Life," other figures in the major poems, and especially important is its
role in *The Cenci*.

Are driven, like ghosts from an enchanter fleeing. . . .
                                            (1-3)

The wind is given the characteristics of an agent that will
send "the leaves dead" to their doom, and the inversion here
places the emphasis on that doom. Rapidly, the remainder of
the first section develops the wind's spirit and its power to
effect change, but the wind itself never becomes an observa-
ble being, as are the leaves, which appear as a physical
reality. Since the "unseen presence" that the narrator tries
to define must remain metaphysical, mysterious, occult, the
fallen leaves are translated into "ghosts from an enchanter
fleeing." Within the first three lines, the rapid accumulation
of attributes like "wild," 'breath of Autumn's being," "un-
seen presence," and "enchanter" are attempts to penetrate
the essence of an indefinable power whose source, as al-
ready noted, is the mind.[37] What the narrator does, of
course, is objectify his own imaginative powers, for the
reader becomes aware that the wind and all things connected
with it derive their reality from the poetic sensibility.

Though associated with the Gothic tradition, the images
quoted do not attempt to create psychological states of fear
or horror; instead they are vehicles for transmitting suspense
and awe that, in turn, suggest the metaphysical structure
supporting the poem. For example, the interaction of the
"ghosts" and the "enchanter" is extended as the leaves, the
"pestilence-stricken multitudes" (5), are laid to rest, "each
like a corpse within its grave" (8), by the wind, the "de-
stroyer and preserver" (14). Personification of the wind and
the leaves reflects the whole process of inspiration and its
ability to revitalize the imagination; thus, when the first

-----

[37]After discussing Shelley's early involvment with the Gothic, Railo continues,
"In the feeling for nature displayed in his subsequent life-work he casts off the
fetters of tradition and becomes the great singer of the sea, the west wind, and the
crystalline ether. . . . It is not impossible, however, that terror-romanticism gave
the first impulse to that freedom from all concreteness in the presentment of nature
that later characterizes his imagination." (p. 155).

section ends with the plea, "hear, oh, hear!" (14), we see the pattern whereby the opening address to the wind and the concluding appeal to its informing powers provide a tight sonnetlike frame for the section and one that will be repeated to accommodate the entire poem. Furthermore, the terrifying qualities associated with the west wind suggest the haunting figure of the conventional Gothic hero-villain and his role of inspiring fear and wonder, although, in this case, the effects will be beneficial, for his potential energies for destruction become cleansing and curative.

As has been pointed out by other scholars,[38] earth, air, and water are, respectively, the central concerns of the first three sections of the poem; and after the narrator describes the wind's effect on the earth, he carries the major metaphor and its characteristics developed in section I over into section II. Here, the Gothic imagery and the thought pattern associated with the air closely parallel the former section:

> Thou on whose stream, mid the steep sky's commotion,
> Loose clouds like earth's decaying leaves are shed,
> Shook from the tangled boughs of Heaven and Ocean,
>
> Angels of rain and lightning: there are spread
> On the blue surface of thine aery surge,
> Like the bright hair uplifted from the head
>
> Of some fierce Maenad, even from the dim verge
> Of the horizon to the zenith's height,
> The locks of the approaching storm. Thou dirge
>
> Of the dying year, to which this closing night
> Will be the dome of a vast sepulchre,

---

[38]See Bloom's analysis of the "Ode to the West Wind," in *Shelley's Mythmaking*, for one of the best lengthy discussions available. Also, Judith Chernaik's *The Lyrics of Shelley* (Cleveland, Ohio, 1972) is helpful; see especially pp. 9-26.

Vaulted with all thy congregated might
Of vapours, from whose solid atmosphere
Black rain, and fire, and hail will burst: oh, hear!

(15-28)

The "breath of Autumn's being" is now the "stream" and acts upon the "loose clouds" in the same manner that it did upon the "decaying leaves." Still an indefinable power, the wind's reality is depicted through various concrete or visible forms such as leaves or clouds, which are respectively compared to "pestilence-stricken multitudes" and "angels of rain and lightning." Also, the "dark wintry bed" and "corpse within its grave" align with "dying year" and "dome of a vast sepulchre." Tumultuous and foreboding impressions alarm the senses and create a tension that increases as the different elements fall victim to the wind. Even much of the color imagery is indirectly repeated: "Yellow, and black, and pale, and hectic red" leaves reinforce the threatening "black rain, and fire, and hail" from the clouds. Finally, the section ends with the same helpless plea, "oh, hear!" as before. What we are interested in at this point is not simply consistency of imagistic association and thought pattern, but especially the mysterious, menacing tone that persists. Shelley's intention seems to be that of creating a cataclysmic atmosphere for use as a necessary binding agent through the first three sections of the poem. Shortly, this intention will be explored.

In the third section, the wind's force comes to bear on the element of water: "Thou who didst waken from his summer dreams / The blue Mediterranean" (29-30) and "Thou / For whose path the Atlantic's level powers / Cleave themselves into chasms" (36-38). Shelley's major circle of physical relationships is complete; the poet's vision draws together earth, sky, and sea as individual entities, but all directed by the compelling energies of an "unseen presence." Maintaining

the parallel with the leaves and clouds, the third section
continues:

> . . . while far below
> The sea-blooms and the oozy woods which wear
> The sapless foliage of the ocean, know
>
>
> Thy voice, and suddenly grow gray with fear,
> And tremble and despoil themselves: oh, hear!
>
> (38-42)

The section contains images of "old places and towers"(33)
and ocean "chasms" that are associated with "oozy
woods" which, like leaves and clouds, "tremble and despoil
themselves" before the wind's force. Again, major and
minor imagery supports the poet's intention of describing
the fearsome agent of the wind. From external phenomena,
the poet gathers impressions that resemble the state of his
own mind, his own creative sterility, and through the third
invocation, "oh, hear!" he begs the wind to inspire his
creative energies much as the "wingèd seeds" (7) in section I
will inspire a new birth in the spring.

The overall logic of the first three sections has been aimed
at developing two levels of personification. On the one hand,
the physical imagery of leaves, clouds, and waves con-
cretizes and gives life to the scene before us, and the reader
recognizes that the imagery is designed to clarify and stress
the idea of helplessness before brute power. On the other
hand, personification works on a metaphysical level to
define the abstract power acting on physical reality. To
grapple with the problem of presenting the inspirational qual-
ity of the wind, Shelley distinguishes passive from active
characteristics in the scene before the narrator as they mir-

ror those same characteristics in his mind.[39]

An active agent that resembles the Gothic villain, the wind is personified as "Wild Spirit," "enchanter," "destroyer and preserver," and "congregated might." As previously suggested, the apocalyptic tone engenders a state not so much of fear as of awe before this scene of cosmic energy. Even the quality of the recipients of this energy, the "pestilence-stricken multitudes" or the "aery surge" that resembles the hair of a "fierce Maenad," helps control the mood and support the sense of mystery and demonic force.[40] Confronting the threatening scene before him, the narrator repeatedly implores the wind to hear him, thus assuming the same passive relationship to the wind that the leaves, clouds, and waves have.

The fourth section seeks the poet's participation in the wind's power, as his plea becomes more demonstrative and particular:

> Oh, lift me as a wave, a leaf, a cloud!
> I fall upon the thorns of life! I bleed!
>
> A heavy weight of hours has chained and bowed
> One too like thee: tameless, and swift, and proud.
>
>   (53-56)

---

[39]An analysis by Professor Schulze helps us to understand Shelley's practice of personification: "Shelley's characters are almost always more than personifications. Their actions tend to stand for principles of action, but only to the degree that these principles are patterns of motivation whose actual fate is undetermined. They are patterns of process. The distinction here is clearly one of perspective and emphasis, but it is as important to Shelley's theory as his organic vocabulary. He wants to stress a progressive pattern in which character is modified as it is developed, but modified from within, as well as from without. Action is seen as the progressive identification of character. Its beginning is the exposition of undetermined energies, usually involving opposition or conflict; its middle is the struggle or quest to unify or clarify these energies; its end is the illumination of character through the fate it had shaped." *Shelley's Theory of Poetry* (The Hague, 1966), p. 200.

[40]See Rieger, p. 174, for a statement on the demonic influences in the "Ode to the West Wind."

He begs for inspiration because life's experiences, "a heavy weight of hours," has clouded his poetic impulses. His loss of imaginative faculty is equivalent to the apparent death of hope, as he indicates in the line "I fall upon the thorns of life! I bleed!" By personifying the wind and making it a cleansing force, the poet hopes to resurrect his dormant faculties. What was originally seen as threatening and destructive—a villain image—has now been translated into a sublime and beneficial experience that aids the imagination: "the valid animation of natural objects, traditionally treated as one form of the rhetorical device of prosopopoeia, or personification, now came to be a major index to the sovereign faculty of imagination, and almost in itself a sufficient criterion of the highest poetry."[41] In the mature poetry, Shelley's use of personification becomes a dynamic, existential willing forth of creative possibilities.

All forms of imagery and personification unite behind a rush of poetic inspiration in the fifth section of the poem. The plaintive note "oh, hear!" of the early sections is completely lost when the poet uses imperative verbs like "make," "be," "drive," and "scatter." The wind has indeed inspired the poet to take command of his vision and ordered it to specific thematic ends:

> Be thou, Spirit fierce,
> My spirit! Be thou me, impetuous one!
>
> Drive my dead thoughts over the universe
> Like withered leaves to quicken a new birth!
> And, by the incantation of this verse,
>
> Scatter, as from an unextinguished hearth
> Ashes and sparks, my words among mankind!
> Be through my lips to unawakened earth

---

[41]M. H. Abrams, *The Mirror and the Lamp* (New York , 1958), p. 55.

The trumpet of a prophecy! O, Wind,
If Winter comes, can Spring be far behind?

(61-70)

The "Wild Spirit," "leaves dead," and "wingèd seeds" of section I have become "Spirit fierce, / My spirit," "dead thoughts," and "the trumpet of a prophecy" in section V. The poem consistently drives toward the realization of the poetic vision through an elaborate series of images and personification, so that "the trumpet of a prophecy" is inspiration, rebirth, and hope that grow out of sinister and intimidating backgrounds. Now, the poet is a promethean light-bringer, a teacher and prophet who orders his physical and inspirational experience for the betterment of man: "Scatter, as from an unextinguished hearth / Ashes and sparks, my words among mankind!" The task of the poetic vision is to bring inspiration to "unawakened earth," to inform it of its potential for good, for "the Romantic poet is a part of a total process, engaged with and united to a creative power greater than his own because it includes his own."[42] And much of this process is illustrated by indicating, through imagery and personification, the Gothic sensibility within the poem and its psychological value in achieving certain ends: out of disruption and pending chaos, Shelley is able to receive stimulation and thus awaken energies that, in his eyes, depend on intricate connections between destructive and creative impulses.

In fact, the few poems that I wish to use as examples to show how Gothic elements enter into a work but then disappear from its central spirit are all dependent on the mastery of the creative over the destructive temper. In the next three poems, my emphasis will confine itself to the presentation of the hero-villain background in the poems and how this divided figure, as Robert Hume noted earlier, loses his Gothic qualities and becomes a Romantic hero.

---

[42]Northrop Frye, *Romanticism Reconsidered* (New York, 1963), p. 14.

III

In *Adonais* (1821), a masterful use of the Wandering Jew figure and the quest-curse convention develops one of the poem's central themes. That one can be his own tyrant and victim simultaneously finds explicit statement in the following passage, which, it can be argued, metaphorically represents the rest of the poem:

> Midst others of less note, came one frail Form,
> A phantom among men; companionless
> As the last cloud of an expiring storm
> Whose thunder is its knell; he, as I guess,
> Had gazed on Nature's naked loveliness,
> Actaeon-like, and now he fled astray
> With feeble steps o'er the world's wilderness
> And his own thoughts, along that rugged way,
> Pursued, like raging hounds, their father and their prey.
>
> (271-79)

One easily marks Ginotti, Wolfstein, Verezzi, Ahasuerus (of *Queen Mab*, not of *Hellas*), the Poet, and the Prince as precursors to this "phantom among men," but the precision of technique and pattern of idea in the passage are remarkable for uniting the Gothic sensibility with an older tradition—that of the classical. Shelley balances abstract and general images with a particular classical myth that underlines his intention: the indefinite "one frail Form," "phantom," "companionless," "last cloud," "expiring storm," "thunder," and "knell" create a mood of dissolution and hopelessness that the narrator then attributes to a psychological, a spiritual circumstance that compares to the specific myth of Actaeon and Artemis. The passage functions admirably in support of the poem's major theme that the "companionless" creative imagination wanders about feebly and hunted by the tyranny of the external world or by the haunting quality of the imagination's ideal vision,

"Nature's naked loveliness." Thus, the author's clarity of imagery here precisely delineates, through tokens of the external world, facets of the mind: "we can . . . suppose from his practice in *Adonais* that he considered imagery a form of communication in which a fusion of figurative and descriptive expression works to harmonize physical with moral or metaphysical levels of awareness."[43]

In keeping with the pastoral elegy convention, the poem arrives at a point where the soul of Adonais is seen as having ascended to the realm of the eternal, and the mourners can cease their lamenting. In death, Adonais is freed from the crass world; instead, we, the living, must continue to face the experiences of life that kill the spirit:

> 'Tis we, who lost in stormy visions, keep
> With phantoms an unprofitable strife,
> And in mad trance, strike with our spirit's knife
> Invulnerable nothings.—We decay
> Like corpses in a charnel; fear and grief
> Convulse us and consume us day by day,
> And cold hopes swarm like worms within our living clay.
>
> (345-51)

There is no difficulty in seeing how this wholly Gothic picture of confused passions and spiritual corruption—"cold hopes swarm like worms within our living clay"—serves the purpose of opposing the worlds of the flesh and the spirit, the pedestrian and the imaginative. Shelley is attempting to depict a psychological demise founded on wild, unprofitable human strife and discontent that bespeak a living death. But it is obvious from the conclusion to the poem that the Gothic spirit must give way to an affirmative, creative vision that does not seek "corpses in a charnel" but, rather "the abode where the Eternal are" (495). In this poem, then, the Gothic world is represented by the flesh and its corruptive charac-

---

[43]Schulze, p. 185.

teristics, while the ideal world is that of the spirit and its permanent qualities.

Only the idea of the quest-curse convention and the means by which Shelley resolves it hold great interest for us when we turn to *Epipsychidion* (1821). The second section of the poem (190-387) distinctly echoes *Alastor* and a few other poems with heroes akin to the Poet:

> There was a Being whom my spirit oft
> Met on its visioned wanderings, far aloft,
> In the clear golden prime of my youth's dawn,
> Upon the fairy isles of sunny lawn,
> Amid the enchanted mountains, and the caves
> Of divine sleep, and on the air-like waves
> Of wonder-level dream, whose tremulous floor
> Paved her light steps;—on an imagined shore,
> Under the gray beak of some promontory
> She met me, robed in such exceeding glory,
> That I beheld her not.
>
>   (190-200)

The narrator continues to elaborate on various aspects of this enchanting being until he finally realizes that "her Spirit was the harmony of truth" (216). Again one finds repeated the idea of the youthful search for knowledge or beauty suddenly culminating in a kind of miraculous recognition, and the thought, "I beheld her not," suggests a subtle warning to the reader that the "veilèd maid" of *Alastor* hovers behind these lines.

Immediately after the narrator's vision of truth, his quest begins:

> Then, from the caverns of my dreamy youth
> I spring, as one sandalled with plumes of fire,
> And towards the lodestar of my one desire,
> I flitted, like a dizzy moth, whose flight
> Is as a dead leaf's in the owlet light,
> When it would seek in Hesper's setting sphere

A radiant death, a fiery sepulchre,
As if it were a lamp of earthly flame.—

(217-24)

The excellent comparison between "Hesper's setting sphere" (love) and "a lamp of earthly flame" (a form resembling fire as we know it) implies the divide between the ideal and the real, the impossible and the possible, and the human propensity to confound the two. Through simile, Shelley presents the elusive concept that confronts the seeker: "as one sandalled with plumes of fire" and "like a dizzy moth" the obsessed narrator rushes toward his "radiant death," "a fiery sepulchre." The idea refuses simple comparison because it would be erroneous to think of purely mental concepts as having one form, one identity —exactly the mistake that the Poet in *Alastor* makes—and simile helps maintain the distance between what is and what seems.

The frenzied quest that develops within the poem is the most distinct sign presented of Gothic sensibility: the narrator's search takes him from one disappointing love affair to another, and each individual attempt to concretize his vision results in the same bitter confusion of the real and the ideal. Finally, through his mad quest, the narrator learns the necessary distinction between his vision and those who seem to embody it. He comes to see that "man cannot contemplate one object of Love and try to make it the only representation of the whole. He thereby simply chains himself to a single inadequate figure."[44] At that point, Emily, "this soul out of my soul" (238), symbolically unites his mind and his heart.

Clearly, Shelley wishes to indicate that the narrator in *Epipsychidion* had discovered a truth denied to the Poet in *Alastor*: one must bring his ideal, his abstraction, into a

---

[44]Milton Wilson, *Shelley's Later Poetry* (New York, 1959), p. 226.

focus that is realizable. Emily, whose "spirit was the harmony of truth," is real as well as ideal because she concretizes the abstraction of love, whereas the Poet's "veilèd maid" remains an abstraction that cannot be realized and thus leads him to his death. *Epipsychidion* not only offers a more complex quest-curse situation than that found in *Alastor*, but also resolves the philosophic question that the poems share: the comparatively self-centered, naïve psychology of the Poet is unable to objectify his experience, falls into error, and persists in it, but the narrator in the later poem errs, comes, through "grief and shame" (322) because of his false attempts to find the ideal, to recognize his mistake, and creates a union of the ideal and the real through deeper knowledge of the self. In this poem, Gothic trappings have become very tenuous indeed (though there does appear a considerable amount of atmospheric imagery, especially during the narrator's search from one love affair to the other), but purposely so, for the protagonist's Gothic quest must end in order that the true nature of love be realized.

More explicitly than any other work, *Prometheus Unbound* (1818-19) indicates the process whereby Gothic elements disappear. Shelley initiates the action of the play by presenting it in a barren setting of icy rocks, a ravine, a precipice, and darkness that suggests the Gothic mind at work (though, symbolically, morning is almost at hand). Prometheus describes the scene about him:

> The crawling glaciers pierce me with the spears
> Of their moon-freezing crystals, the bright chains
> Eat with their burning cold into my bones.
> Heaven's wingèd hound, polluting from thy [Jupiter's] lips
> His beak in poison not his own, tears up
> My heart; and shapeless sights come wandering by,
> The ghastly people of the realm of dream,
> Mocking me: and the Earthquake-fiends are charged
> To wrench the rivets from my quivering wounds
> When the rocks split and close again behind:
> While from their loud abysses howling throng

> The genii of the storm, urging the rage
> Of whirlwind, and afflict me with keen hail.
>
>   (I.31-43)

It is out of this description of physical and mental suffering that the Gothic sensibility gains such prominence in the early part of the play. Prometheus faces the task of eliminating the destructive sensibility at work by subduing the chaos in his own mind and thus in the world. The images in the quoted passage are particularly revealing because of what they say about the protagonist's mental relationship with the outer world: "Since Shelley believes that the mind is as real as the external world, and of the same order of reality, he often begins with subjective ideas and states and clothes them with natural and concrete imagery."[45] Besides Gothic imagery, one also finds another convention in use that appears in Shelley's early work.

The quest that Prometheus originally undertakes is designed to bring knowledge to man, which, in turn, will set him free from the tryranny of ignorance, superstitition, and the power of the gods. If acquired, knowledge—self-knowledge, that is—would then permit man to discard the perennial afflictions of suspicion, fear, hate, and other common forms of destruction. But because Prometheus is cursed by ignorance of his own weaknesses, he is at first unable to achieve his quest, and thus remains in bondage to forces of evil, symbolized by Jupiter.

As the poem begins, it is ironically apparent that Prometheus is a captive of exactly those states of mind that he seeks to abolish from the world. Chained to a mountain in the Caucasus, he is still under the illusion, three thousand years after his original act of defiance, that his oppressor exists outside of himself; thus he addresses Jupiter in the following terms:

---

[45]Fogle, p. 224.

"Monarch of Gods and Daemons. . .

. . . .

         regard this Earth
Made multitudinous with thy slaves, whom thou
Requitest for knee-worship, prayer, and praise,
And toil, and hecatombs of broken hearts,
With fear and self-contempt and barren hope.
Whilst me, who am thy foe, eyeless in hate,
Hast thou made reign and triumph, to thy scorn
O'er mine own misery and thy vain revenge."

            (I. 1-11)

From this passage we see that the center of the Titan's concern, despite his claim to high purpose, is his own proud hatred of Jupiter. The quest he undertook has been abortive since he himself is not yet ready for the freedom he desires for others: blinded by hatred and rebellious pride, he has yet to realize that it is not knowledge of the world but knowledge of self that is the key to reaching his goal.

  Cursed by Jupiter, the Titan in return imposes a curse on his master, not realizing that by doing so he curses himself. Both Jupiter and Prometheus enter into a psychologically intricate pattern of tyranny and servitude: they are both tyrants and both slaves at the same time, for their mutually dependent relationship is based on revenge and hate. Centuries later, through suffering and reflection on the nature of his fate, Prometheus begins to have doubts about his attitude of hate and begs that the words of his curse be repeated to him so that he can reconsider them. The Phantasm of Jupiter appears and echoes the words of the Titan:

 Fiend, I defy thee! with a calm, fixed mind,
  All that thou canst inflict I bid thee do;
 Foul tyrant both of Gods and Human-kind,
  One only being shalt thou not subdue.

         (I. 262-65)

and his defiant pride and hatred lead to:

I curse thee! let a sufferer's curse
Clamp thee, his torturer, like remorse;
Till thine Infinity shall be
A robe of envenomed agony;
And thine Omnipotence a crown of pain,
To cling like burning gold round thy dissolving brain.

(I.286-91)[46]

Though on a much more sophisticated level, Prometheus's mocking and vengeful attitude reminds one of Zastrozzi's pose at the time of his execution. The Gothic hero-villain is noble and attractive in his refusal to bow before unjust and evil authority, but he is also morally weak and unattractive in his inability to rise above the vindictive characteristics of that authority. Competing for attention, his affirmative and negative features embroil him in a vicious circle that leads to destruction.

But Prometheus's moral revolution is at hand; and after he hears the curse repeated, his sincere sorrow and pity for Jupiter, who, because he is the principle of oppression and evil, must remain forever bound to hatred, insures the Titan's progress toward self-discovery. When the hero-villain's moral sensibilities show him his weakness, his error of hate, when he repents of his evil and retracts his curse, then he rises out of the circle of ignorance:

It doth repent me: words are quick and vain;
Grief for awhile is blind, and so was mine.
I wish no living thing to suffer pain.

(I.303-5)

No longer a captive of hate, Prometheus's conquest of self-

---

[46]In his "Essay on Christianity" (1812-15?), Shelley described the relationship between a divine being and man in these terms: "Mankind, transmitting from generation to generation the horrible legacy of accumulated vengeances and pursuing with the feelings of duty the misery of their fellow beings, have not failed to attribute to the universal cause a character analogous with their own." *Prose*, p. 206.

knowledge is achieved, and, simultaneously, through the aid of Asia and Demogorgon, his curse is lifted and the quest that man obtain "Life, Joy, Empire, and Victory" (IV. 578) is complete.

Early in the play, the Titan's struggle ends, for the Prometheus of the first act is a very different character from that in the remainder of the drama. Before the retraction of the curse, he embodies all the attributes of the Gothic hero-villain:

> Almighty, had I deigned to share the shame
> Of thine ill tyranny, and hung not here
> Nailed to this wall of eagle-baffling mountain,
> Black, wintry, dead, unmeasured; without herb,
> Insect, or beast, or shape or sound of life.
> Ah me! alas, pain, pain ever, for ever!
> No change, no pause, no hope! Yet I endure.
> I ask the Earth, have not the mountains felt?
> I ask you Heaven, the all-beholding Sun,
> Has it not seen? The Sea, in storm or calm,
> Heaven's ever-changing Shadow, spread below,
> Have its deaf waves not heard my agony?
> Ah me! alas, pain, pain ever, for ever!
>
>   (I.18-30)

One sees that Prometheus's haggard external form is accompanied by the pose of defiance; his quest to bring knowledge carries the curse of self-ignorance, both of which move from external to internal manifestations; he is filled with doubt, gloom, and melancholy; an isolated figure, his challenge to authority moves on a worldly and spiritual plane; metaphysical forms and mysterious forces of nature are his constant companions; and lastly, his quest produces a spiritual tension and awe because of the suprahuman task the Titan faces. After his moral victory over Jupiter, however, Prometheus completely loses his villainous Gothic characteristics and is transmuted into a noble hero. In acting out the process of this transmutation, he erases the dual nature of the Gothic hero-villain convention, the conflict between head and heart, the tendency toward destruction.[47] Clearly a member of the same family of hero-villains as Zastrozzi, Ginotti, Wolfstein, the Poet of *Alastor*, and the protagonists of many other mature works, Prometheus goes far beyond them in his response to the quest-curse situation, and by doing so, he indicates a pattern of self-knowledge that harmoniously balances personal and universal, physical and metaphysical experience. With the death of the Gothic villain, the Romantic hero is born.

---

[47]In the study of *The Cenci* that follows, we will see that the Gothic hero-villain convention also dies, but for **exactly opposite reasons**.

4

The Gothic Sensibility
in *The Cenci*

It is entirely appropriate that my study of Gothic elements in Shelley's works conclude with an examination of *The Cenci* (1819). This drama includes not only obvious aspects of the Gothic tradition[1] but also major themes that we have seen in previous chapters. As well, the psychological complexity that I have been stressing in the mature works is brought to a fine edge in the play and delicately completes, by emphasizing the dark compartments of the mind, the deep insight into human nature that Shelley possessed. My primary approach to the play follows from the Gothic foundations already established; that is, seeing how they underlie the drama and analyzing whatever new ideas about understanding Shelley's work that they may suggest.

---

[1]One should note the strain of literary scholarship that accentuates or mentions the Elizabethan and classical influences on *The Cenci*. See particularly Carlos Baker, *Shelley's Major Poetry* (Princeton, 1948), pp. 150-51; E. S. Bates, *A Study of Shelley's Drama*, The Cenci (New York, 1908), pp. 52-57; D. L. Clark, "Shelley and Shakespeare," *PMLA* 54 (1939): 277-86; S. R. Watson, "*Othello* and *The Cenci*," *PMLA* 55 (1940): 611-14; Benjamin Kurtz, *The Pursuit of Death* (London, 1933), pp. 191-92; and Bertrand Evans, *Gothic Drama From Walpole To Shelley* (Berkeley, 1947), pp. 230-31. In no way do I wish to dispute these studies; on the contrary, they aid my interests, but few of the above scholars have given careful, if any, consideration to Gothic elements in the play.

My calling *The Cenci* Gothic is determined by a number of considerations that deal with conventional interests in theme, story, setting, and characterization. My argument will develop around these considerations, but, besides keeping in mind Shelley's other works, I will emphasize the fact that drama imposes certain demands and opens up many possibilities not available to other genres. For example, in essentially narrative and expository forms of prose and poetry, the reader enjoys a detachment, an objective stance, that drama purposely tries to abolish. By seeking to involve the audience directly, drama's existential quality uses devices to implant a dialectic so that, for the most part, a character must bring himself into being. Whatever exposition of human failings or accomplishments a drama presents, whatever theme we might find in a play, or whatever we might find out about ourselves by witnessing a human situation onstage, one of the main points of this chapter is that the inherently dramatic nature of the Gothic tradition is, for Shelley, better revealed in the work under discussion than in any other early or late production of his.

In the preface to *The Cenci*, Shelley mentions the manuscript containing the history of that unfortunate family; then he goes on:

> Such a story, if told so as to present to the reader all the feelings of those who once acted it, their hopes and fears, their confidences and misgivings, their various interests, passions, and opinions, acting upon and with each other, yet all conspiring to one tremendous end, would be as a light to make apparent some of the most dark and secret caverns of the human heart.[2]

If we compare this statement of "didactic" intention—even though Shelley's dedication of the play to Leigh Hunt denies such an intention—with a passage from *A Defence of Poetry*, we should get a notion of Shelley's complex understanding

---

[2]*The Complete Poetical Works of Percy Bysshe Shelley*, ed. Thomas Hutchinson (London, 1943), pp. 275-76.

of tragedy and what he hopes to accomplish through the play:

> It is difficult to define pleasure in its highest sense—the definition involving a number of apparent paradoxes. For, from an inexplicable defect of harmony in the constitution of human nature, the pain of the inferior is frequently connected with the pleasures of the superior portions of our being. Sorrow, terror, anguish, despair itself are often the chosen expressions of an approximation to the highest good. Our sympathy in tragic fiction depends on this principle: tragedy delights by affording a shadow of the pleasure which exists in pain.[3]

That there truly are "dark and secret caverns of the human heart" and that an audience derives great pleasure from seeing them exposed are undeniable propositions. That the Gothic tradition devoted its principal energies to exploiting the former because of the latter is equally undeniable, and a serious analysis of Gothic materials (or of tragedy in general) must continually focus on the combination of pain and pleasure. One need not infer from the above that Shelley was a sadist or reveling in the sensationalist ventures of his youth when he wrote his "dark drama"; rather, he is portraying that which is all too apparent in the human situation, that which he preferred to call "sad reality": "*The Cenci* is a strangely disquieting vision of evil in which the characters peer into themselves and greet the depths which they discover with various degrees of horror, fascination, and acceptance."[4]

A list of the more common Gothic elements in *The Cenci* that help to activate the concept of the "horribly beautiful"

---

[3]*Prose*, p. 292. Shelley's conception of tragedy can be compared, in many respects, to Nietzsche's argument in "The Birth of Tragedy"; see especially pp. 216-18 and 221-29, *The Philosophy of Nietzsche* (New York, n.d.).

[4]Milton Wilson, *Shelley's Later Poetry* (New York, 1959), p. 90.

would have to include the following: a villain,[5] an abused heroine who becomes a villain, a conniving priest, religious inquisitional figures, a rape-incest situation, parricide, a torture chamber and dungeons, a Gothic palace and distant castle, the curse and revenge motifs, horror, terror, gloom, and melancholy. We note that there are no supernatual occurrences or any deep mysteries in the play, but there are religious, supernatural backgrounds and dramatic suspense, which compensate for more usual flamboyant Gothic characteristics. Also, the scene is set quite far in the past (the end of the sixteenth century) and thus initially we are able to accept the bizarre circumstances because they are so distant from us. All of these features, even down to the final unmasking of the Count's murderers and preparation for their execution, are quite obvious and what we might call external properties of the Gothic tradititon.

But when we turn toward more speculative, philosophical, or psychological issues, which can be termed internal matters of the Gothic, then we discover not only the theme of tyranny (mental, physical, and spiritual), but also the much more complicated idea of ambiguity and ambivalence that we saw in *Alastor* and elsewhere: because of an originally ambiguous situation, our final response is ambivalent. Going far beyond *Alastor*, however, *The Cenci* does not stop at ambivalence but instead insists that we push on to grapple with the process by which we might delude ourselves into accepting an ambivalent position. This form of argument, of dialectic, a kind of casuistry through which an individual or a society can manipulate all forms of thought or action to justify whatever particular ends he or it might have in mind, will be the center of our attention.

---

[5]It is tempting to see the Count as a hero-villain, and from one point of view this is defensible: in a patriarchal society, the measure of fear and respect that a person like the Count demands makes him a kind of hero. However, this argument is sophistic because it contributes nothing to our understanding of his character and actions.

Perhaps the best place to begin a discussion of the text itself, in terms of external Gothic particulars, is with the ending remarks in Shelley's preface:

> The Cenci Palace is of great extent; and though in part modernized, there yet remains a vast and gloomy pile of feudal architecture in the same state as during the dreadful scenes which are the subject of this tragedy. . . . One of the gates of the Palace formed of immense stones and leading through a passage, dark and lofty and opening into gloomy subterranean chambers, struck me particularly.[6]

One easily sees how this entrance conveniently becomes a merging of physical and psychological reality, and the ensuing darkness indeed envelops both body and soul. Throughout the play, as the scenes move from the Cenci Palace to the Castle of Petrella, the Hall of Justice, and the prison, the overall effect is one of confinement, oppression, and gloom. The various apartments, the garden at the Palace, the ramparts at Petrella, and the cell and hall of the prison are stages for the presentation of schemes, deceit, and the corruption of the human spirit; there is a constant interplay of external setting and internal human motivation. Even Beatrice's description of the scene at which the murder of the Count is first attempted carefully mirrors aspects of her own soul and of her ultimate destiny:

> "But I remember
> Two miles on this side of the fort, the road
> Crosses a deep ravine; 'tis rough and narrow,
> And winds with short turns down the precipice;
> And in its depth there is a mighty rock,
> Which has, from unimaginable years,
> Sustained itself with terror and with toil
> Over a gulf, and with the agony
> With which it clings seems slowly coming down;

---

[6]*Poems*, p. 278.

Even as a wretched soul hour after hour,
Clings to the mass of life; yet clinging, leans;
And leaning, makes more dark the dread abyss
In which it fears to fall: beneath this crag
Huge as despair, as if in weariness,
The melancholy mountain yawns . . . below,
You hear but see not an impetuous torrent
Raging among the caverns, and a bridge
Crosses the chasm; and high above there grow,
With intersecting trunks, from crag to crag,
Cedars, and yews, and pines; whose tangled hair
Is matted in one solid roof of shade
By the dark ivy's twine. At noonday here
'Tis twilight, and at sunset blackest night.''
                                              (III.i.243-65)

Since these lines come after her father has raped her, it is apparent that her tortured body and mind are reflected in the scene she pictures, and her soul, "a mighty rock," a "crag / Huge as despair," is almost ready to topple into "the dread abyss." Moreover, the "cedars, and yews, and pines" resemble the chaos within her that makes "sunset blackest night."[7] There can be little doubt that Shelley practices great economy—a precision in the use of imagery and tone—to create certain psychologically dramatic units that press relentlessly toward the dark center of the play. Another example occurs when the Count tells his wife that they will leave the Palace and go to the Castle of Petrella. There he can better pursue his designs to seduce Beatrice repeatedly and thus slowly corrupt her spirit:

". . . I will take you where you may persuade
The stones you tread on to deliver you:

---

[7]Though Shelley refers to this passage as one of the few instances of "what is commonly called mere poetry," in the play, his remark that immediately follows informs us of the intention behind such a passage: "In a dramatic composition the imagery and the passion should interpenetrate one another, the former being reserved simply for the full development and illustration of the latter." *Poems*, p. 277.

For men shall there be none but those who dare
All things—not question that which I command.
On Wednesday next I shall set out: you know
That savage rock, the Castle of Petrella:
'Tis safely walled, and moated round about:
Its dungeons underground, and its thick towers
Never told tales; though they have heard and seen
What might make dumb things speak."

(II.i.163-72)

The imagery of the castle focuses our attention on the intricate web of tyranny and oppression that is central to the Count's nature and to the meaning of the play. The Count's remark "not question that which I command" is a direct response to Lucretia and Beatrice's moves, however gentle and justified, to dispute his authority: he will stop rebellion and satisfy his insidious desires at the Castle, "that savage rock," "walled," "moated," with "dungeons underground" and "thick towers." Images of despotism and suppression occur regularly when the Count speaks, and the above external Gothic features accord with his character.

It is hardly necessary to quote other passages, such as the one that takes place at the beginning of Act III, just after Beatrice has been raped, or the scene when the Count is murdered, or the one in the prison cell, to emphasize the point about the intimate relationship between Gothic imagery and the human mind. These images are not mere appendages or melodramatic clothing designed for sensational effect; they are crucial to the accurate delineation of human character as it appears in this play. In *Gothic Drama from Walpole to Shelley*, Bertrand Evans states why *The Cenci* partakes of the Gothic tradition, but also why such a play as this helped destroy that tradition:

> The theme of persecution aligns it with Gothic tradition in both fiction and drama. The principal characters are Gothic types idealized. Some scenes, especially those before and after Cenci's attack on Beatrice, would fit unaltered into a Gothic

play. Several descriptive passages paint settings which were favorites of Gothic writers after Mrs. Radcliffe. But Shelley's unawareness of the contemporary theater, his intimacy with dramatic masterpieces, and his poetic power prevented full achievement of his lower aim to write a play "of a more popular kind." Aided by Shakespearean and classical drama, his art elevated the Gothic to such an unprecedented height that, though it achieved triumph, it suffered obscuration.[8]

Evans's point serves us well here because it indicates how far we can expect to go with the argument for Gothic elements in the play before we are forced to translate these elements into higher objectives than those common to the Gothic school. What should most deeply interest us, though, is the process through which this conversion takes place. Imagery offered one way to approach the issue. I hope to combine other external characteristics of the Gothic with internal matters so that the process of transformation is more succinctly and effectively traced.

The hero-villain concept, which has been basic to my complete study, varies in *The Cenci* so that its main energies are not directed to what has formely been called the quest-curse motif. Instead, upon investigating the nature of the diverse characters, we find that they are all weak or villainous or both. Beatrice is the only one who can properly be called heroic, but even she finally becomes a villain. The larger issue we are seeking, though, is the combination of themes that determines the motives and actions of the main characters. Essentially, the themes of tyranny and corruption are what I wish to develop now, for they decide other considerations in the play. Also, these themes will lead most naturally to an analysis of the principle of casuistry, which Shelley saw as the real tragedy in Beatrice's experience and which I will extend to the whole drama, after seeing it in operation through three characters. But first the major themes should be noted.

---

[8]Evans, p. 232.

The play begins with Cardinal Camillo saying to Count Cenci,

> "That matter of the murder is hushed up
> If you consent to yield his Holiness
> Your fief that lies beyond the Pincian gate."
>
> (I.i.1-3)

Within three lines, Shelley abruptly introduces his audience to murder, religious tyranny, corruption, the power of money or possessions, and an atmosphere of secrecy and intrigue.[9] All of these elements expand and merge with other forces, until we realize that the whole society is engaged in and bound together by a monstrous pattern of deceit and self-gain: murder is a common occurrence that can easily be excused by the church if proper payment is made; authority extends from God to the church and then to the head of the family and is misused to maintain order; order is maintained not for the sake of protection and the enforcement of justice but for the sake of the few who exercise control; and lastly, tyranny and corruption have reached the point where the society is so impregnated with their effects and so confused by their close association with attitudes of righteousness that it can no longer distinguish right from wrong. This last consideration is perhaps the most insidious line of thought in the play, for it implies that all actions can be justified; it does away with all objective standards and suggests that subjective interest is the only measure of conduct. The end result, of course, is the destruction of the human spirit and a return to the jungle. The above three lines offer us a clue for examining the corruption generally present in the play's individual characters and situations, but they do so without imposing a simple formula.

---

[9]References to material goods are, directly or indirectly, extraordinarily present in *The Cenci* and we see that wealth is a determining factor for much of the dark action in the play. The urge to dominate, to possess, has a great deal to do with the physical and psychological identity of the Gothic villain.

The Count is an excellent picture of the Gothic villain and a precise indicator of the pervasive villainy in society. We need only return to Shelley's first novel to find his counterpart. "He is a development of one of Shelley's earliest fascinations, for he is a Zastrozzi matured."[10] As in previous chapters, our main interest lies in the development, the maturing, of the Gothic villain convention, and from the point of view of revenge and defiance, Zastrozzi and Cenci are comparable, yet distinctions must be made.

We will recall that the ethic of revenge Zastrozzi practiced demanded that the victim's body and his soul be destroyed; thus, Verezzi had to be driven to despair and then commit suicide. Here, the villain's intention—to avenge his mother's disgrace—is quite straightforward, and his plan of destruction is simple. The Count's motives—sadism, avarice, maintenance of authority—are much more complex than those of Zastrozzi, but the essential plan of destruction holds: Cenci will subject his daughter's body to his infamous sexual demands so that her spirit is destroyed and her will perverted. But whereas Zastrozzi merely wished to eradicate his enemy, the Count is more calculatingly evil because he seeks to preserve Beatrice and make her into a living image of his own vileness. Cenci's plan of revenge, therefore, satisfies his lust, his avarice (he will not have to provide a dowry), and his drive to dominate the only member of his family whose willpower compares with his own and whose purity exposes his depravity. Also, the type of defiance these villains exhibit is comparable, and at this juncture we can add the figure of Ginotti as well: Zastrozzi mocks his inquisitors and laughs at the hell that awaits him as the novel ends; Ginotti denies God and sells his soul to the Devil; and the Count, though constantly invoking the image of God when it is convenient, answers his wife's pleas that he revoke his curse on Beatrice by saying, while motioning to-

---

[10]Kurtz, p. 191.

ward heaven, " 'He does His will, I mine!' " (IV.i.139). The audience knows that such an act of hubris will surely cause the gods to enact their will . . . to the detriment of the profaner. Zastrozzi and Ginotti, however, are so obvious and bold-faced in the way they shake their fists at heaven that our interest soon wanes. But the Count's defiance leads us to the principle behind his actions that has critical importance for our study.

There are two major agents that the Count can defy—God and the Church—and, except in the example noted above, he seldom challenges either of them with complete impunity; instead of foolishly mocking powers beyond his control, he manipulates them by invoking either custom or money. For example, as head of the family, Cenci uses the traditional image of God as father for a basis of domination over his wife and children; he finds it useful to appear religious in a conventional sense because the image of God serves certain ends. In relation to the church, the count is capable of buying his way out of most difficulties, and this gives him a high degree of influence over the only agent he might fear directly. He knows very well how far he can go to satisfy his self-interest because he understands the self-interest of others and has discovered he can use it to his advantage. When Cardinal Camillo threatens him, Cenci answers urbanely,

> "Nay this is idle:—We should know each other.
> As to my character for what men call crime
> Seeing I please my senses as I list,
> And vindicate that right with force or guile,
> It is a public matter, and I care not
> If I discuss it with you. I may speak
> Alike to you and my own conscious heart—
> For you give out that you have half reformed me,
> Therefore strong vanity will keep you silent
> If fear should not; both will, I do not doubt."
> (I.i.66-76)

Unfortunately, the Count is right, and it is his ability to analyze his own motives and the motives of others that gives him such demonic powers. His logic moves from the careful examination of his particular character to the general character of men:

> "All men delight in sensual luxury,
> All men enjoy revenge; and most exult
> Over the torture they can never feel—
> Flattering their secret peace with others' pain."
>   (I.i.77-80)

Needless to say, not only is the Count indicating the principle of tragedy that Shelley raises in the "Defence," but also the process by which he excuses himself; that is, the pursuit of self-interest that is common to all men. The great difference between Cenci and other men is that, where they dream, he acts. He is quick to admit his villainy and equally quick to excuse it by stating that his motives are the same as everyone's, but simply carried to their full conclusion. Thus, he puts himself above the law, above any reproach, by becoming a law unto himself. Through self-analysis and a fine dissection of human motives, the Count turns all questions of conscience into ambiguous propositions; he becomes a casuist and twists God, church, and family into the service of his evil ends. The Gothic hero-villain is often noted as placing himself beyond the confines of law and society, but in few works does the process by which he accomplishes this feat come out so clearly as it does in *The Cenci*.

Another aspect of the Count's character to be closely marked is his plot to master Beatrice sexually. It is true that "in *The Cenci* the fierceness of algolagnic sensibility is clearly marked . . .,"[11] but this, too, in the Count's sophistic reasoning, can be excused and justified. The first hint of his

---

[11]Devendra P. Varma, *The Gothic Flame* (London, 1957), p. 199.

designs to perform an act of extreme disgust comes after the Cardinal's warning and the advice to calm down; the Count replies:

> "Ay, we must all grow old—
> And but that there yet remains a deed to act
> Whose horror might make sharp an appetite
> Duller than mine—I'd do—I know not what."
>
> (I.i.99-102)

It is not common lust that motivates him, but a complex combination of perversity, tyranny, iconoclasm, and self-justification:

> "Nous sommes des dieux" declared Sade's characters. The perverse Saint-Fond in *Juliette* spoke just like Cenci when he boasted that there was no ecstasy like that "que l'on goûte en se livrant à cette divine infamie." Nor was the behaviour of Sade's "heroes" towards their relations so very different from the threats of Cenci against his daughter, which he obviouly uttered with the intention of feeling "délicieusement chatouillé" by breaking laws which men consider sacred.[12]

The enormity of his criminal plan to rape Beatrice and then bring her to the point of corruption where she will enter freely into an incestuous union shocks even the conscience of the Count,[13] but since he already admits to an evil nature and since Beatrice is a disobedient and insolent daughter, he is able to brace himself up and proceed in his plan. First he informs her of his intentions (between Act I, scene iii and Act II), but her strong character repulses him. The following day, however, her fearful look lets him know that her will is beginning to break. He pursues his advantage, and by the beginning of Act III he has already possessed her body. The next step involves the move to the castle, where the gradual

---

[12]Mario Praz, *The Romantic Agony* (London, 1933), p. 114.
[13]See particularly I.ii.136-38; I.iii.169-72; II.i.123-28 and 181-93; and IV.i.177-82.

corruption of Beatrice's spirit is to take place. In Act IV, scene i, the Count even goes so far as to tell his wife of his scheme:

> "I will drag her, step by step,
> Through infamies unheard of among men:
> She shall stand shelterless in the broad noon
> Of public scorn, for acts blazoned abroad,
> One among which shall be . . . What? Canst thou guess?
> She shall become (for what she most abhors
> Shall have a fascination to entrap
> Her loathing will) to her own conscious self
> All she appears to others; and when dead,
> As she shall die unshrived and unforgiven,
> A rebel to her father and her God,
> Her corpse shall be the terror of the earth;
> Her spirit shall approach the throne of God
> Plague-spotted with my curses. I will make
> Body and soul a monstrous lump of ruin."
>
> (IV.i.80-95)

Cenci's mind is a difficult maze, indeed. He seeks such complete destruction and revenge that we wonder what Beatrice could have done to provoke him to such threat and to the extreme curses that immediately follow. Carlos Baker gives three conditions for the Count's behavior: "a perverted sexual drive," avarice, and vengeance.[14] I do not argue with these observations, which Baker carefully discusses, but my Gothic interest moves me to emphasize the combination of the sexual drive and vengeance (avarice is such a common feature of the society and Cenci so sees his wealth as the only real weapon to maintain his power over others besides Beatrice that I will not bother to consider this motive in examining his relationship to her).

In the previous chapter, I used Shelley's poem on the Medusa image to comment on the Gothic tradition. The

---

[14]Baker, *Shelley's Major Poetry*, pp. 144-45.

immediately preceding quotations from Varma and Praz point to the idea that the Count's vicious threats and curses are based on sadism and a delight in horror, but we can best understand these elements by seeing his deep-seated fear of Beatrice, the Medusa image in his world of evil.

At the banquet that the Count gives to celebrate the death of his two sons, Beatrice openly unmasks his villainy to the guests. She is the only one with courage enough to identify him for what he is. After the guests have left, he strikes back:

> "Thou painted viper!
> Beast that thou art! Fair and yet terrible!
> I know a charm shall make thee meek and tame,
> Now get thee from my sight!"
>
> (I.iii.165-68)

She is fair because she is innocent, lovely, and the only person equal to him; she is terrible because these very qualities are the greatest threat imaginable to his world. Her goodness and moral courage are direct opposites of the tryannical self-image that the Count must retain. He is fascinated by her, but he knows that he must destroy her or she will destroy him. As Whitman points out: "In Count Cenci, then, Shelley has embodied the major evils which he sees as the curse of mankind, the negation of all that is good, and which he almost always associated with the tryant-figure: hate as opposed to love; the impulse to destroy overcoming the impulse to create; and most important, the will to power and domination, denying man's greatest good, his freedom."[15] Given the image of evil he presents, his hate and revenge are natural forms of protection against love, or, as he calls his daughter, "this my bane and my disease, / Whose sight infects and poisons me" (IV.i.118-19). Furthermore, we misunderstand the nature both of Beatrice and of the

---

[15]Robert F. Whitman, 'Beatrice's 'Pernicious Mistake' in *The Cenci*," *PMLA* 74 (1959): 251.

Count if we fail to see the fatal attraction, in turn, his principle of evil has for her. Thus, Cenci is not insane nor inexplicably perverse when he says:

> "I do not feel as if I were a man,
> But like a fiend appointed to chastise
> The offences of some unremembered world.
> My blood is running up and down my veins;
> A fearful pleasure makes it prick and tingle;
> I feel a giddy sickness of strange awe;
> My heart is beating with an expectation
> Of horrid joy."
>
> (IV.i.160-67)

We cannot be sure if the "unremembered world" is that of innocence, of Beatrice, or the threat to the Count's own conscience—his self-identity—but we can agree with Kurtz that a "horrid joy," ". . . a tragic union of loveliness and death, like that of the Medusa, is the heart of the poem."[16]

Behind all of the Count's thoughts and actions is an abiding tyrannical psychology that directs his twisted logic to suppress his daughter's rebelliousness on the one hand and destroy her innocence on the other. Insofar as tyranny grows out of fear, out of a threat to one's self, it is obvious that the Count can justify his actions on many grounds, even though the base for each of his complex attitudes is always founded on evil principles. Our response to him is in no way ambivalent, but we can see the twisting of logic by which he creates ambiguous situations: in his world, Beatrice is guilty of being good, and if he is to survive, good must become evil. Wilson explains it thus: "By his act of incest Cenci will force Beatrice to turn her stern gaze inward, to recognize the contamination within her and to realize that she is what she contemplates."[17]

---

[16]Kurtz, p. 190.

[17]Wilson, p. 84. Wilson's analysis of the principle of casuistry and how it leads to "ingrown love" is the longest and best one available for our interests; see particularly pp. 78-92.

   The familiar Gothic convention of the conniving priest
forms a handy link between the casuistry of the Count and
that of Beatrice, between inherent villainy and acquired
villainy. Orsino has nowhere near the evil nature that the
Count has, but neither is he near Beatrice's original inno-
cence. More than anything else, his persistent trait is oppor-
tunism, and to be a successful opportunist, casuistry is es-
sential. The first words Beatrice speaks drive our attention
to the center of his character: "Pervert not truth, / Orsino"
(I.ii.1-2). And a few lines after these she adds, "You have a
sly, equivocating vein / That suits me not" (I.ii.28-29). The
irony in these lines as they apply to Beatrice's later actions
cannot be taken up here, but it is quite apparent that she
quickly distinguishes elements in the character of others that
allows the audience a basis for critical judgment. We now
know what to expect from Orsino.
   The Gothic tradition took a great interest in the Machiavel-
lian activities that a priest could perform. As a religious
figure, he had ready access to possibilities denied to others:
he could serve in both temporal and spiritual realms; he was
an excellent purveyor of secret messages between con-
spirators; he could be a reconciler between parties of op-
posed interest; and he was usually considered above suspi-
cion. Not all of these apply to Orsino, but as a catalyst in the
plot to murder the Count, he is crucial. Beatrice, Lucretia,
and Giacomo all have pressing reasons for Cenci's death,
and Orsino, to win Beatrice and her dowry, plays the role of
Iago to urge the unspoken thought of parricide into the open.
A practiced casuist, he understands well the habit among the
Cencis:

> "It fortunately serves my close designs
> That 'tis a trick of this same family
> To analyse their own and other minds.
> Such self-anatomy shall teach the will
> Dangerous secrets: for it tempts our powers,
> Knowing what must be thought, and may be done,

Into the depth of darkest purposes:
So Cenci fell into the pit; even I
Since Beatrice unveiled me to myself,
And made me shrink from what I cannot shun,
Show a poor figure to my own esteem,
To which I grow half reconciled. I'll do
As little mischief as I can; that thought
Shall fee the accuser conscience."

(II.ii.107-19)

And with such anatomizing as this, Orsino "fell into the pit."
He deceives himself by using the same process as others use
to "fee the accuser conscience." Even before Beatrice is
raped, Orsino tries to make Giacomo voice the word murder,
but unsuccessfully. Finally, the mother rather clumsily
blurts out what all are thinking and Orsino takes care of the
details of the projected murder, with alacrity.

Through all of his machinations, we see the same essential
process of self-justification as that which answered the
Count's needs. True, Orsino is not so evil as the Count, but
he probably could be if necessary.

> Shelley's interest in the motive of Orsino suggests another
> reason for the rather long part he has in the play. Orsino acted
> according to the dictates of his ambition, his love for Beatrice,
> and, most significantly, of the Church. Ambition and selfish
> love lead him to assist the parricides. He deserts them just as the
> Church deserts them. It is he who withholds the petition from
> the Pope. It is in him that we see an emblem of the corrupt
> ecclesiastical hierarchy, indifferent to suffering in its deter-
> mined veneration for the patriarchal order. Orsino's behavior is
> the "modus vivendi" required in this degenerate period of
> history.[18]

Certainly the part of this statement that could apply to Car-
dinal Camillo and the Pope extends the casuistic principle

---

[18]Paul Smith, "Restless Casuistry: Shelley's Composition of *The Cenci*," *K-SJ*
13 (1965): 81.

outward and even heavenward, as Beatrice suggests in the last scene of the play (V.iv.77-89). But our interest in Orsino must return to more restricted grounds so that the comparison to Cenci is, in casuistic terminology, "justified."

After the Count's murder has been discovered and Lucretia and Beatrice apprehended, the action finds Orsino and Giacomo turning against one another:

> ORSINO. "You cannot say
> I urged you to the deed."
>   GIACOMO. "O, had I never
> Found in thy smooth and ready countenance
> The mirror of my darkest thoughts; hadst thou
> Never with hints and questions made me look
> Upon the monster of my thought until
> It grew familiar to desire. . ."[19]
>   ORSINO. " 'Tis thus
> Men cast the blame of their unprosperous acts
> Upon the abettors of their own resolve;
> Or anything but their weak, guilty selves."
>   (V.i.18-27)

And the dialectic of excusing oneself goes on until no one is guilty, because all thoughts and actions have become ambiguous. I agree that these characters are not equally guilty, but, again, I emphasize the point that self-interest leads all the conspirators to enter into the same process of self-deception. If conscience becomes solely a plaything for the analytic powers of the mind, then all can be permitted. When Giacomo tells Orsino that they must give themselves up and share the guilt for the murder, along with Lucretia and Beatrice, Orsino tricks him into becoming a device to aid in the priest's escape. Orsino then soliloquizes on his role in the whole affair by using the same particular "I" in the general

---

[19]We note that the mirror idea is used repeatedly in the play, and all the major characters are seen in relation to it. This idea compares with the self-image that was noted earlier in the major poems. See Wilson, pp. 83-85.

"all men" argument that the Count used:

> "I thought to act a solemn comedy
> Upon the painted scene of this new world,
> And to attain my own peculiar ends
> By some such plot of mingled good and ill
> As others weave. . . ."
>
> (V.i.77-81)

We see that if the society in which he lives is based on "my own peculiar ends," then the Count can no more be despised than the priest can: "Orsino, though not a Cenci, has the same moral weakness as the Cenci, the self-analysis which leads him to make the best of his shortcomings, whose deformities gradually become familiar and even attractive to him."[20] And it is exactly on the grounds of "moral weakness" that Orsino bridges the gap between the Count and Beatrice. We have seen a complete villain, a partial villain, and now it is necessary to examine a heroine changed into a villain.

Beatrice stands forth as a fine replica of the conventional Gothic female protagonist, but she is a more intricate combination of two opposed types than was Cythna in *The Revolt of Islam*, who remains a heroine throughout the poem. On the one hand, she reminds us of the loveliness and innocence of Countess Julia in *Zastrozzi* and Eloise in *St. Irvyne*; while on the other hand, she echoes the fatal beauty and duplicity of the former novel's Matilda and the latter's Megalena. We had no difficulty in recognizing the motivations of all four of these early creations, for Shelley conveniently and naively formed his characters into distinct types and colors and moved his chess pieces into simple positions. But our knowledge of life's game is deeply taxed when the diverse pieces merge into one force and move both ways at once, when Julia and Eloise become Matilda and Megalena, when

---

[20]*Poems*, p. 276.

Shelley mixes good and evil into the figure of Beatrice.

To refer once again to the preface of the play, there the author states:

> Undoubtedly, no person can be truly dishonoured by the act of another; and the fit return to make to the most enormous injuries is kindness and forbearance, and a resolution to convert the injurer from his dark passions by peace and love. Revenge, retaliation, atonement, are pernicious mistakes. If Beatrice had thought in this manner she would have been wiser and better; but she would never have been a tragic character.[21]

Since we know that she is a tragic character, our interest must be in the subtle process by which good is initially pushed toward, eagerly embraces, and finally desperately becomes evil. For this chain of physical and psychological events to happen, the heroine must have a tragic flaw, which, of course, always grows out of pride. With Beatrice, the flaw does not appear in the original fact that she lies, enters into the plot to commit parricide, and then is willing to sacrifice a hired assassin to save her own life, but, rather, in her failure to understand what true innocence is. Her soul is not noble enough to realize that, if one is pure, "no person can be truly dishonoured by the act of another." Her pride in her virtue is so great that she, like the Count, will become a law unto herself, and she takes personal revenge for the Count's actions rather than have others outside of her family know that she is stained. Her original sin is inextricably involved with her original goodness, and as her fate works itself out, evil grows from the imperfect innocence of self-love.

I have mentioned Beatrice's admirable ability to stand up to her father's unconscionable tyranny, but it is fascinating to see how innocence and one's pride in it will react with righteous indignation after an attack on the bastion of purity. The following scene comes the day after the Count first made

[21]*Poems*, p. 276.

his vile proposition to Beatrice. She repulsed him, but as she hysterically talks with her step-mother, Lucretia, and her younger brother, Bernardo, the breach in her strength is apparent:

> *(speaking very slowly with forced calmness.)* "It was one word,
>   Mother, one little word;
> One look, one smile. *(Wildly.)* Oh! He has trampled me
> Under his feet, and made the blood stream down
> My pallid cheeks. And he has given us all
> Ditch-water, and the fever-stricken flesh
> Of buffaloes, and bade us eat or starve,
> And we have eaten."
>
> (II.i.63-69)

Shortly thereafter the Count enters and her frightened look tells him that the strength of perfect evil is greater than that of imperfect innocence. Her pride initially keeps her from revealing what the Count has said; she only offers hints of his foul approach, and this same proud reluctance to expose the fact that purity could be spotted in any way whatsoever is the basis for her downfall. Her heroic and potentially villainous qualities are of the same fabric, and this, perhaps more than anything else, is the "sad reality" that Shelley reveals. It is not my intention to be overly harsh in interpreting Beatrice's character—she has certainly been wronged, but the temptation to excuse her must be resisted, for that avenue leads to the principle of self-deception about which the play revolves.

Just as the Count felt Beatrice to be a threat to his tyranny of evil, so she feels him to threaten her whole kingdom of innocence. I have tried to indicate that if that kindgom were secure enough, she could not be "dishonoured," but when the Count looks upon her, she can only respond with "O that the earth would gape! Hide me, O God!" (II.i.111). Recalling Beatrice's earlier firmness, we are left with the question, why does not innocence resist evil again? It must be that innocence is willing to risk its virtue rather than, because of pride, tell the world that an attack on it is imminent. When the physical attack on her chastity is complete, Beatrice cannot answer with "peace and love," as Shelley suggests, but only with madness and panic:

> "My God!
> The beautiful blue heaven is flecked with blood!
> The sunshine on the floor is black! The air
> Is changed to vapours such as the dead breathe
> In charnel pits! Pah! I am choked! There creeps
> A clinging, black, contaminating mist
> About me . . . 'tis substantial, heavy, thick,
> I cannot pluck it from me, for it glues
> My fingers and my limbs to one another,
> And eats into my sinews, and dissolves
> My flesh to a pollution, poisoning
> The subtle, pure, and inmost spirit of life!"
>
> (III.i.12-23)

A few lines after this vivid description of how purity reacts to being polluted—obviously characterized by distinct Gothic imagery— the thought of parricide passes through Beatrice's mind. Her metamorphosis gathers speed when Orsino arrives, but not before we are given conclusive evidence of her misguided pride, or her imperfect innocence. Orsino suggests,

> "Accuse him of the deed, and let the law
> Avenge thee."
> BEATRICE. "Oh, ice-hearted counsellor!
> If I could find a word that might make known
> The crime of my destroyer; and that done,
> My tongue should like a knife tear out the secret
> Which cankers my heart's core; ay, lay all bare
> So that my unpolluted fame should be
> With vilest gossips a stale mouthed story;
> A mock, a byword, an astonishment."
>
> (III.i.152-60)

And for the sake of her "unpolluted fame," Beatrice takes the necessary step toward murder—a "pernicious mistake." A casuistic discussion then takes place among Beatrice, Lucretia, and Orsino, so that all the conspirators come to feel completely justified; Giacomo soon joins the plot, and the engine of revenge is put into motion. I agree that "Beatrice falls through the perversion of her character towards that of the Count's. He forces her, through overt act and continuous psychological pressure, to accept his premises on the nature of desire and will. These are the premises of selfhood, which finds integrity in nothing,"[22] but I add that her excessive pride makes the Count's actions possible.

The psychological stages that Beatrice successively manifests are: offensive innocence (early attack on her father's tyranny), outrage (her father's proposal), defensive fear (the day following the proposal), disgust and derangement (after she has been raped), offensive revenge (the plot of parricide), and then a complicated series of mental maneuvers to avoid capture and execution, none of which is successful. Our major concern, though, is with the principle of casuistry that possesses her mind after the decision to murder the Count is made. Urgency compels Beatrice to become hard, calculating, and even more self-righteous in evil than she was in innocence. For example, when the hired murderers hesitate at a noise, she mocks them with, "Ye conscience-stricken cravens, rock to rest / Your baby hearts' " (IV.ii.39-40). And when the two men enter the sleeping Count's room but return with excuses for being unable to kill him, she shames them into doing the deed:

> "Miserable slaves!
> Where, if ye dare not kill a sleeping man,
> Found ye the boldness to return to me
> With such a deed undone? Base palterers!
> Cowards and traitors! Why, the very conscience

---

[22]Earl J. Schulze, *Shelley's Theory of Poetry* (The Hague, 1966), pp. 203-4.

Which ye would sell for gold and for revenge
Is an equivocation: it sleeps over
A thousand daily acts disgracing men;
And when a deed where mercy insults Heaven. . . .
Why do I talk? [*Snatching a dagger from one of them and
    raising it.*]
            Hadst thou a tongue to say,
'She murdered her own father!'—I must do it!
But never dream ye shall outlive him long!''
                                        (IV.iii.22-33)

Finally, while the assassins are murdering the Count,
Beatrice says to Lucretia,

            "How pale thou art!"
We do but that which 'twere a deadly crime
To leave undone.
        LUCRETIA."Would it were done!"
        BEATRICE."Even whilst
That doubt is passing through your mind, the world
Is conscious of a change. Darkness and Hell
Have swallowed up the vapour they sent forth
To blacken the sweet light of life. My breath
Comes, methinks, lighter, and the jellied blood
Runs freely through my veins!"
                                        (IV.iii.36-44)

Beatrice is as adroit at manipulating others, justifying the
crime,[23] and psychologically "rejoicing" in it as her father
was in his schemes. Also, it is interesting that she accepts
Zastrozzi's ethic of revenge, for she permits her father's
body and soul to be destroyed, since the old man was mur-
dered unshrived,[24] which is a condition he had forecast for

---

[23]It is important to remember that all parties to the crime express deep reserva-
tions and even shock at the thought of parricide, which informs us that it was not
undertaken with free conscience. Their hesitation is somewhat similar to the
Count's reservations about raping Beatrice.

[24]For further parallels between the Count and Beatrice, though not with the
emphasis given in this study, see Wilson, pp. 84-88.

her. Beatrice, in her defense, revenge, and justification, has reversed the conditions of innocence and love, and now she must follow her new path with full commitment.

The cruel irony of the Pope's legate, with orders to apprehend and execute Cenci, arriving immediately after the murder and arresting the accomplices instead, forms the set of circumstances that drives Beatrice to utter desperation. She sacrifices all principles of innocence and becomes a more formidable practitioner of casuistry than even the Count and Orsino were. In his discussion of *The Cenci*, Carlos Baker notes a relationship between it and *Prometheus Unbound* that can help us see how far Beatrice has strayed from her ideals:

> The contrast between *Prometheus* and *The Cenci* is the contrast between what might be and what is. As in the *Prometheus*, Shelley subjected his central figure to all the diabolical rapier-thrusts and bludgeonings that mind and flesh could bear. But this time the reaction was more complicated, as the individual human being is always more complicated than any symbol which can be devised for him. This time no ethical conversion renovated the world. Instead, under indignities of the most horrible kind, a gentle and innocent girl was turned into an efficient machine of vengeance, coolly planning, imperiously executing, denying her part in, and at last calmly dying for the murder of her father.[25]

And the last part of Act IV and all of Act V is a careful exposure of the magnitude of Beatrice's fall: once caught, she uses every trick imaginable to escape her impending doom. When the legate tells Lucretia and Beatrice they must go to Rome to be investigated, the latter's response is a masterful piece of indignation, deceit, and unwitting irony:

---

[25]Baker, *Shelley's Major Poetry*, p. 142. Since my approach has been that Beatrice is not really the innocent victim that most scholars claim, even from the beginning of the play, I can accept Baker's interpretation only in part.

"Guilty! Who dares talk of guilt! My Lord,
I am more innocent of parricide
Than is a child born fatherless. . .Dear mother,
Your gentleness and patience are no shield
For this keen-judging world, this two-edged lie,
Which seems, but is not."

                                               (IV.iv.111-16)

The whole question of appearance and reality, as in *Alastor*
and in most of the other mature poems we have studied, is
the issue that Shelley stresses to develop Beatrice's tragedy.
She, unfortunately, knows what the issue is and then pro-
ceeds to be victimized by appearance, the very falsity she
condemns; she accepts the rules of play in "this keen-
judging world, this two-edged lie," and, of course, the great
temptation for the audience is to agree with her, to remember
her innocence only to justify her guilt. The shadow of the
Count's evil looms even larger behind her words and ac-
tions.

Particularly in the trial scenes of Act V does casuistry
become the principal force that binds the drama together. All
begins in ambiguity and suspicion, but after a series of con-
fessions, betrayals, and self-justifications, we realize that
Shelley does not intend an ambivalent response on our part
to Beatrice, nor to the world in which her tragedy takes
place: we are to see, through Beatrice in particular and
through the society in general, that self-interest leads to the
loss of ideals, which for the Cencis, insures corruption and
spiritual and physical death.

We cannot really be surprised when Beatrice once again
manipulates Marzio, one of the hired assassins, into shoul-
dering full responsibility for the murder, thereby absolving
the instigators of the plot. She simply accepts her father's
logic of self-interest and pursues it to a bitter conclusion.
When Marzio is tortured and confesses to the murder, he
also implicates the others. Beatrice asks:

"What evil have we done thee? I, alas!

Have lived but on this earth a few sad years,
And so my lot was ordered, that a father
First turned the moments of awakening life
To drops, each poisoning youth's sweet hope; and then
Stabbed with one blow my everlasting peace
Which sleeps within the core of the heart's heart;
But the wound was not mortal; so my hate
Became the only worship I could lift
To our great father, who in pity and love,
Armed thee, as thou dost say, to cut him off;
And thus his wrong becomes my accusation;
And art thou the accuser? If thou hopest
Mercy in heaven, show justice upon earth:
Worse than a bloody hand is a hard heart.''
                                        (V.ii.118-33)

And her stern gaze and heartrending words to him force her
new victim to perjure himself, accept full blame for the
crime, and exonerate the others. The above passage con-
tains much of Beatrice's history: her innocence, the rape,
her pride in "untainted fame," her derangement, hate, re-
ligious righteousness, and finally her "hard heart" that dares
to speak of justice and mercy. The last line is probably the
most ironic and tragic one of all—she begins to resemble her
father more and more, and Marzio goes willingly to his death
on the "two-edged lie" of casuistry.

But the judges are not satisfied, and the torture of
Giacomo and Lucretia brings out the truth, at which point
Beatrice attacks them, the judges, and even God. She con-
tinues to justify herself, but the death sentence faces the
culprits. Cardinal Camillo—though corrupt, perhaps the
least villainous of any—tries to intercede for them. The
Pope, however, is adamant that they die, and his explanation
is another exercise in the vicious circle of casuistry that
permeates the play:

    "Parricide grows so rife
That soon, for some just cause no doubt, the young

Will strangle us all, dozing in our chairs.
Authority, and power, and hoary hair
Are grown crimes capital."

(V.iv.20-24)

We can see how the whole structure of society is based on a
principle of authority that can easily be converted into
tyranny so that God, the Pope, and the Count himself stand
above reproach, regardless of what they may do. And Bea-
trice, certainly a victim of that tyranny, "would have been
wiser and better," as Shelley argues, if she had used her
innocence to rise above it. Instead, her moral fibre gives way
to the conditions of life that surround her:

> The critical discomfiture over Beatrice's conduct in the fifth
> act, like the sneaking suspicion that Count Cenci is far too black
> to be credible, rest upon a failure to appreciate the intricacies of
> Shelley's intention. In brief that intention is to display the
> perhaps inevitable corruption of human saintliness by the con-
> spiracy of social circumstances and the continued operation of a
> vindictive tyranny.[26]

It is thus that Shelley's drama goes beyond the conventional
Gothic interest in horror and terror for their own sake and
indicates the major themes that preoccupied him throughout
his brief career: the confusion of appearance and reality, the
essence of virtue and love, individual and social tyranny, the
corruption and degradation of the human spirit, and the
difficulty of finding meaning and peace in life, to name a few.
Certainly Beatrice's character incorporates all the essential
human possibilities noted during this study: she could have
been promethean and finally won her battle for physical and
spiritual life, but she chose to be a true Cenci, which could
only guarantee tragedy.

The most horrible vision that Shelley presents to embody
this tragedy occurs to Beatrice shortly after Camillo has

---

[26]Baker, *Shelley's Major Poetry*, pp. 147-48.

brought the Pope's refusal of pardon; she says,

> "If there should be
> No God, no Heaven, no Earth in the void world;
> The wide, gray, lampless, deep, unpeopled world!
> If all things then should be . . . my father's spirit,
> His eye, his voice, his touch surrounding me;
> The atmosphere and breath of my dead life!
> If sometimes, as a shape more like himself,
> Even the form which tortured me on earth,
> Masked in gray hairs and wrinkles, he should come
> And wind me in his hellish arms, and fix
> His eyes on mine, and drag me down, down, down!
> For was he not alone omnipotent
> On Earth, and ever present? Even though dead,
> Does not his spirit live in all that breathe,
> And work for me and mine still the same ruin,
> Scorn, pain, despair?
>
> (V.iv.57-72)

No direr fate could happen to Beatrice than that she be bound to her father eternally—an incestuous union of innocence and evil. At last the Count has won, for, as he said, " 'she shall grope through a bewildering mist / Of horror' " (II.i.184-85) and " 'become (for what she most abhors / Shall have a fascination to entrap / Her loathing will) to her own conscious self / All she appears to others' " (IV.i.85-88). After her completely despairful vision, she is left feeling empty and cold. She has no remorse, no pacifying hopes for heaven, and no illusions about what the gossips will say of her "unpolluted fame." She is wholly resigned to her death and portrays a mixture of helplessness and nobility. The best words one can think of as an epitaph to her sad history are found in her own stoic remark,

> "What 'twas weak to do,
> 'Tis weaker to lament, once being done. . . ."
>
> (V.ii.111-12)

My study has been relentless in trying to come to grips with the question of Beatrice's innocence, and often I have possibly been too hard on her. But the issue is central not only to the play but also to the mainstream of Shelley's thought, and thus we must pursue her character a bit further, especially in relation to the play's preface:

> It is in the restless and anatomizing casuistry with which men seek the justification of Beatrice, yet feel that she has done what needs justification; it is in the superstitious horror with which they contemplate alike her wrongs and their revenge, that the dramatic character of what she did and suffered, consists.[27]

As an audience, therefore, our response is ambivalent because of the ambiguous circumstances surrounding her acts: we know she is truly innocent and is provoked into the heinous deeds she commits, but, on the other hand, her inexcusable deceit and ultmate spiritual wretchedness (as opposed, for example, to Hamlet's tragedy) force us to conclude that she truly is guilty. In the process of trying to explain our ambivalence, we, too, become casuists and feel that no human being could undergo the humiliation and torture that Beatrice does without acting as she did. Thus, we justify her and our own emotional response at the same time "so that the pleasure which arises from the poetry which exists in these tempestuous sufferings and crimes may mitigate the pain of the contemplation of the moral deformity from which they spring."[28] Our casuistry subtly leads us back into the vicious Cenci world where everything can be explained and, in one way or another, excused—including the characters of the Count, Orsino, and Beatrice.[29] We

---

[27]*Poems*, pp. 276-77.

[28]*Poems*, p. 276.

[29]In tragedy, one may consider casuistry as a kind of defense mechanism—a desperate effort at rationalization that seeks to make life acceptable in tragic circumstances. In *The Cenci*, however, casuistry goes too far and the alert audience must guard against confusing casuistry in the play and the critical doctrine of casuistry as valid response to tragedy. We must disclaim the type of casuistry that surrounds the Cencis.

have a sense of being trapped at the end of the play, for if all characters are guilty (though, of course, not in the same way: the Count's casuistry is based on a deep will to evil that is the essence of his being, whereas Beatrice's casuistry is initially a sincere desire to right an evil situation and only later deforms her character completely; we should see that evil is an accident and not the essence of her character), then to what standard can we turn for a source of values? If the world of the Cencis—God, Church, society, and family—is totally corrupt, then the audience is forced to respond by rejecting that world and the principle of tyranny, corruption, and casuistry that infects it. In turn, we are implicitly asked to accept the state of ideal innocence that Beatrice could have represented.

The Cenci follows the same basic argument as that of "The Triumph of Life": the people who follow "the Car of Life" do not "know themselves"; they have lost their ideals because their experience has led them to accept appearance rather than reality. The self-analysis that the Cencis practiced did not insure a knowledge of ideals but, rather, one of evils, and since their realization is founded on self-interest, on self-love, they are assured of a tragic conclusion, in Shelley's view. For these reasons, *Prometheus Unbound* is exactly the reverse of *The Cenci* (which was written in a period between the third and fourth acts of *Prometheus*): the Titan, through his sufferings, comes to understand his ideal self, but Beatrice's sufferings force her away from her ideal self; the love of the former hero brings about regeneration and salvation, while the hate of the latter engenders destruction and perdition. Again in his preface, Shelley asks us to choose the ideal way:

The highest moral purpose aimed at in the highest species of the drama, is the teaching the human heart, through its sympathies and antipathies, the knowledge of itself; in proportion to the possession of which knowledge, every human being is wise, just, sincere, tolerant and kind.[30]

Obviously, these characteristics apply more to Prometheus than they do to Beatrice, and as we reflect back on the unhappy fates of the Poet in *Alastor*, Mahmud in *Hellas*, Rousseau in "The Triumph of Life," and Beatrice herself, it is apparent that they experienced a confusion or a loss of their ideals. Opposed to them stand the narrators of *Alastor*, the "Hymn to Intellectual Beauty," *Adonais*, *Epipsychidion*, "Ode to the West Wind," the hero and heroine of *The Revolt of Islam*, and *Prometheus Unbound*. Throughout Shelley's major poetry, the quest has constantly been for the ideal vision, and the curse that necessarily accompanies the quest is the human propensity to confound the ideal by accepting the world of appearances.

In *The Cenci*, the full acceptance of appearances and the use of casuistry to justify them indicate the demise of the human spirit, the approach of darkness and chaos; essentially, the Gothic tradition can be viewed as an attempt to explore the persistent conflicts that rage within man that lead to this demise. I have tried to argue that theme, story, setting, and principal characters in *The Cenci* are as much a part of the Gothic tradition as they are in line with Shelley's central poetic and philosophic concerns. My argument in dealing with the play and with Shelley's major poems has been that the conventions found in *Zastrozzi* and *St. Irvyne* have been refined to the point where device serves intention with extraordinary felicity, and the Gothic sensibility became a vehicle of great range and precision to portray Shelley's unbending commitment to examine the light and the dark side of man's complex nature.

On a larger scale, the Gothic tradition was useful to Shelley because, by its nature, it reflected many of the attitudes coursing through Europe in the late eighteenth and early nineteenth centuries:

---

[30]*Poems*, p. 276.

the relationship between tormented villain and oppressed maiden is a more complex projection of the European state of mind during a period which saw the overthrow of a good part of western civilization's traditional structure and system of values. The villain and maiden between them may be said to represent two facets of the human spirit's sense of its imprisonment and perversion by an old, tyrannical order: its awareness that it had been bound from without by absolutist institutions, and twisted within by the attitudes these same insititutions engendered.[31]

The Romantic urge to break from the social, political, and philosophical restrictions of the eighteenth century needed some invention like the Gothic to probe levels of human experience that had been generally blocked since the time of the Elizabethans. The new freedom that the Gothic romance provided, in terms of the idea of the hero-villain, the emancipated woman, the escape from the particulars of time and space, the supernatural, and the diabolic side of man's character, distinctly bespeaks the psychological and imaginative energies current at the time. These energies directed themselves at every major institution, including those of marriage, the family, the church, the government, and class structure. Thus it is true that not only in Shelley's juvenilia but also, and especially, in his most mature work do we discover the presence of a Gothic dark angel. Shelley's vision, in prose and in poetry, is always man-centered, and the Gothic tradition, with its rich possibilities for presenting the ambiguities and struggles within man, becomes a major component of that vision.

---

[31]William F. Axton, in the Introduction to Charles Robert Maturin, *Melmoth the Wanderer* (Lincoln, Neb., 1961), p. x.

Selected Bibliography

Abrams, M. H. *The Mirror and the Lamp: Romantic Theory and the Critical Tradition*. New York: W. W. Norton, 1958.

————.*Natural Supernaturalism: Tradition and Revolution in Romantic Literature*. New York: W. W. Norton, 1971.

Arnold, Matthew. "Shelley," in *Poetry and Criticism of Matthew Arnold*. Edited by A. Dwight Culler. Boston: Houghton Mifflin Company, 1961.

Axton, William F., ed. *Melmoth the Wanderer*. Lincoln, Neb.: University of Nebraska Press, 1961.

Baker, Carlos. *Shelley's Major Poetry: The Fabric of a Vision*. Princeton: Princeton University Press, 1948.

————."Spenser, the 18th Century, and Shelley's *Queen Mab*," *MLQ* 2 (1942): 81-98.

Barnard, Ellsworth. *Shelley's Religion*. Minneapolis: University of Minneapolis Press, 1936.

Barrell, Joseph. *Shelley and the Thought of His Time: A Study in the History of Ideas*. New Haven: Yale University Press, 1947.

Bates, E.S. *A Study of Shelley's Drama, The Cenci*. New York: Macmillan, 1908.

Birkhead, Edith. *The Tale of Terror*. London: Constable and Co., Ltd., 1921.

Bloom, Harold. *Shelley's Mythmaking*. New Haven: Yale University Press, 1959.

————. *Romanticism and Consciousness: Essays in Criticism*.

New York: W. W. Norton, 1970.

Bostetter, E. E. *The Romantic Ventriloquists: Wordsworth, Coleridge, Keats, Shelley, Byron*. Seattle, Wash.: University of Washington Press, 1963.

Brinton, Crane. *The Political Ideas of the English Romanticists*. Ann Arbor, Mich.: The University of Michigan Press, 1966.

Burke, Edmund. *A Philosophical Inquiry into the Origins of Our Ideas of the Sublime and the Beautiful*. Edited by J. T. Boulton. London: Routledge and Kegan Paul, 1958.

Bush, Douglas. *Mythology and the Romantic Tradition in English Poetry*. Cambridge, Mass.: Harvard University Press, 1937.

Butter, Peter H. *Shelley's Idols of the Cave*. Edinburgh: University Press, 1954.

Cameron, Kenneth Neil. "A Major Source of *The Revolt of Islam*," *PMLA* 56 (1941): 175-206.

————."The Political Symbolism of *Prometheus Unbound*," *PMLA* 58 (1943): 728-53.

————."Shelley Scholarship: 1940-1953; A Critical Survey," *K-SJ* 3 (1954): 89-109.

————. *The Young Shelley: Genesis of a Radical*. New York: Collier, 1962.

————, and Frenz Horst. "The Stage History of Shelley's *The Cenci*," *PMLA* 60 (1954): 1080-1105.

Campbell, Olwen W. *Shelley and the Unromantics*. New York: Scribner's, 1924.

Carpenter, Edward, and George Barnefield. *The Psychology of the Poet Shelley*. London: G. Allen and Unwin, 1925.

Chernaik, Judith. *The Lyrics of Shelley*. Cleveland, Ohio: The Press of Case Western Reserve University, 1972.

Chesser, Eustace. *Shelley and Zastrozzi: self-revelation of a neurotic*. London: Gregg/Archive, 1965.

Clark, David Lee. "Shelley and Shakespeare," *PMLA* 54 (1939), 261-87.

Clark, Sir Kenneth. *The Gothic Revival*. London: C. Tinling and Co., Ltd., 1964.

Clayborough, Arthur. *The Grotesque in English Literature*. Oxford: Clarendon Press, 1965.

Collins, Grace Calvert. "Shelley's Treatment of the Legend of the Wandering Jew." Master's Thesis, University of North Carolina, 1961.

Dacre, Charlotte. *Zofloya, or the Moor*. London: The Fortune Press, 1928.

Duerksen, Ronald. *Shelleyan Ideas in Victorian Literature*. The Hague: Mouton and Co., 1966.

Eisinger, Chester E. "The Gothic Spirit in the Forties," in *Pastoral and Romance*. Edited by Eleanor Terry Lincoln. Englewood Cliffs, N. J. : Prentice-Hall Inc., 1969.

Eliade, Mircea. *Myths, Dreams, and Mysteries*. New York: Harper and Row, 1967.

Ellis, F. S. *A Lexical Concordance to the Poetical Works of Percy Bysshe Shelley*. London: B. Quaritch, 1892.

Evans, Bertrand. *Gothic Drama from Walpole to Shelley*. Berkeley: University of California Press, 1947.

Firkins, Oscar. *Power and Elusiveness in Shelley*. Minneapolis: University of Minnesota Press, 1937.

Fogle, Richard H. *The Imagery of Keats and Shelley: A Comparative Study*. Hamden, Conn.: Archon Books, 1962.

————."The Imaginal Design of Shelley's 'Ode to the West Wind,' " *ELH* 15 (1948): 219-26.

Frankl, Paul, *The Gothic: Literary Sources and Interpretations through Eight Centuries*. Princeton: Princeton University Press, 1960.

Frye, Northrop, ed. *Romanticism Reconsidered: Selected Papers from the English Institute*. New York: Columbia University Press, 1963.

Gérard, Albert. "Alastor, or the Spirit of Solipsism," *PQ* 33 (1954): 164-77.

Godwin, William. *Enquiry Concerning Political Justice*, in *Backgrounds of Romanticism*. Edited by Leonard M. Trawick. Bloomington, Ind.: Indiana University Press, 1967.

Grabo, Carl H. *The Magic Plant: The Growth of Shelley's*

Thought. Chapel Hill, N. C.: University of North Carolina Press, 1939.

———. *A Newton Among Poets: Shelley's Use of Science in Prometheus Unbound*. Chapel Hill, N.C.: University of North Carolina Press, 1930.

———. *Prometheus Unbound: An Interpretation*. Chapel Hill, N.C.: University of North Carolina Press, 1935.

Graham, Walter. "Shelley and The Empire of the Nairs," *PMLA* 40 (1925): 881-91.

Halliburton, D. G. "Shelley's 'Gothic' Novels," *K-SJ* 16 (1967): 39-49.

Havens, R. D. "Shelley the Artist," in *The Major English Romantic Poets*. Edited by Clarence D. Thorpe, Carlos Baker, and Bennett Weaver. Carbondale, Ill.: Southern Illinois University Press, 1957.

Heilman, Robert B. "Charlotte Brontë's 'New' Gothic," in *Victorian Literature: Modern Essays in Criticism*. Edited by Austin Wright. New York: Oxford University Press, 1961.

Hildebrand, W. H. *A Study of Alastor*. Kent, Ohio: Kent State University Bulletin, 42, no. II (1954).

Hoffman, H. L. *An Odyssey of the Soul*. New York: Columbia University Press, 1933.

Hughes, A. M. D. *The Nascent Mind of Shelley*. Oxford: Clarendon Press, 1947.

———. "Shelley's *Zastrozzi* and *St. Irvyne*," *MLR* 7 (1912): 54-63.

Hume, Robert D. "Gothic versus Romantic: A Revaluation of the Gothic Novel," *PMLA* 84 (1969): 282-90.

Hungerford, E. B. *Shores of Darkness*. New York: Meridian, 1963.

Ingpen, Roger, and W. E. Peck, eds. *The Complete Works of Percy Bysshe Shelley*. 10 vols. New York: Scribner's, 1926-1930.

Jones, F. L. "*Alastor* Foreshadowed in *St. Irvyne*," *PMLA* 49 (1934): 969-71.

———. "the Inconsistency of Shelley's *Alastor*," *ELH* 13 (1946): 291-99.

————. "The Vision Theme in *Alastor* and Related Works," *SP* 64 (1947), 108-25.

Jeaffreson, J. C. *The Real Shelley: New Views of the Poet's Life*. 2 vols. London: Hurst and Blackett, 1885.

Jung, C. G. *The Basic Writings of C. G. Jung*. Edited by Violet Staub de Laszlo. New York: The Modern Library, 1959.

Kurtz, Benjamin P. *The Pursuit of Death*. London: Oxford University Press, 1933.

Lévy, Maurice. *Le Roman "Gothique" Anglais: 1764-1824*. Toulouse: Association des Publication de La Faculté des Lettres et Science Humaine de Toulouse, 1968.

Lewis, Matthew G. *The Monk*. New York: Grove Press, 1952.

Lovejoy, Arthur O. "The First Gothic Revival and the Return to Nature." *Essays in The History of Ideas*. New York: Capricorn Books, 1960.

McIntyre, Clara F. "The Later Career of the Elizabethan Villain-Hero," *PMLA* 40 (1925): 874-80.

Monk, Samuel H. *The Sublime: A Study of Critical Theories in XVIII-Century England*. Ann Arbor, Mich.: University of Michigan Press, 1960.

Nelson, Lowry, Jr. "Night Thoughts on the Gothic Novel," in *Pastroral and Romance*. Edited by Eleanor Terry Lincoln. Englewood Cliffs, N. J.: Prentice-Hall Inc., 1969.

Nietzsche, Friedrich. *The Philosophy of Nietzsche*. New York: The Modern Library, n.d.

Notopoulos, J. A. *The Platonism of Shelley*. Durham, N.C.: Duke University Press, 1949.

O'Malley, Glenn. *Shelley and Synesthesia*. Evanston, Ill.: Northwestern University Press, 1964.

Penzoldt, Peter. *The Supernatural in Fiction*. London: P. Nevill, 1952.

Praz, Mario. *The Romantic Agony*. London: Oxford University Press, 1933.

Pulos, C. E. *The Deep Truth: A Study of Shelley's Scepticism*. Lincoln, Neb.: University of Nebraska Press, 1962.

Radcliffe, Ann. *The Mysteries of Udolpho*. London: Oxford University Press, 1966.

Railo, Eino. *The Haunted Castle*. New York: Humanities Press, Inc., 1964.

Reiter, Seymour. *A Study of Shelley's Poetry*. Albuquerque, N.M.: University of New Mexico Press, 1967.

Rieger, James. *The Mutiny Within: The Heresies of Percy Bysshe Shelley*. New York: George Braziller, 1967.

Roe, Ivan. *Shelley: The Last Phase*. London: Hutchinson, 1953.

Rogers, Neville. *Shelley at Work: A Critical Inquiry*. Oxford: Clarendon Press, 1956.

Ruskin, John. *Stones of Venice*. 3 vols. London: J. M. Dent & Co., 1907.

Schulze, Earl J. *Shelley's Theory of Poetry: A Reappraisal*. The Hague: Mouton & Co., 1966.

Shelley, Percy Bysshe. *The Complete Poetical Works of Percy Bysshe Shelley*. Edited by Thomas Hutchinson. London: Oxford University Press, 1943.

―――. *The Complete Works of Percy Bysshe Shelley*. Edited by Roger Ingpen and W. E. Peck. 10 vols. New York: Scribner's, 1926-1930.

―――. *The Esdaile Notebook: A Volume of Early Poems*. Edited by K. N. Cameron. New York: Knopf, 1964.

―――. *The Letters of Percy Bysshe Shelley*. Edited by F. L. Jones. 2 vols. Oxford: Clarendon Press, 1964.

―――. *Shelley's Critical Prose*. Edited by Bruce R. McElderry, Jr. Lincoln, Neb.: University of Nebraska Press, 1967.

―――. *Shelley's Prose; or, The Trumpet of a Prophecy*. Edited by David Lee Clark. Albuquerque, N.M.: University of New Mexico Press, 1954.

―――, and Thomas Medwin. *The Wandering Jew*. Edited by Bertram Dobell. London: Reeves and Turner, 1887.

Sickels, Eleanor M. *The Gloomy Egoist: Moods and Themes Of Melancholy from Gray to Keats*. New York: Columbia University Press, 1932.

―――. "Shelley and Charles Brockden Brown," *PMLA*, 45 (1930): 1116-28.

Smith, Paul. "Restless Casuistry: Shelley's Composition of *The Cenci*," *K-SJ* 13 (1965): 78-85.

Solve, M. T. *Shelley: His Theory of Poetry*. New York: Russell & Russell. 1964 [1927].

Spacks, Patricia Meyer. *The Insistence of Horror*. Cambridge Mass.: Harvard University Press, 1962.

Stovall, Floyd. *Desire and Restraint in Shelley*. Durham, N.C.: Duke University Press, 1931.

Summers, Montague. *A Gothic Bibliography*. New York: Russell & Russell, 1964.

———. *The Gothic Quest*. London: Fortune Press, 1938.

Sweet, Henry. "Shelley's Nature Poetry." *The Shelley Society's Papers*, ser. I, no. I, pt. II, pp. 269-324. London: Reeves and Turner, 1891.

Tompkins, Joyce. *The Popular Novel in England 1770-1800*. London: Arthur Barker, Ltd., 1957.

Varma, Devendra P. *The Gothic Flame: Being a History of the Gothic Novel in England*. London: A. Barker, 1957.

Vivante, Leone. *English Poetry*. Carbondale, Ill.: Southern Illinois University Press, 1963.

Walpole, Horace. *The Castle of Ortranto*. New York: Collier Books, 1963.

Wasserman, Earl R. *The Subtler Language: Critical Readings of Neoclassic and Romantic Poems*. Baltimore, Md.: Johns Hopkins Press, 1959.

Watson, S. R. "*Othello* and *The Cenci*," *PMLA* 55 (1940): 611-14.

Weaver, Bennett. "Shelley," in *The English Romantic Poets*. Edited by Thomas M. Raysor. New York: MLA, 1957.

White, Newman Ivey. *Shelley*. 2 vols. New York: Knopf, 1940.

Whitman, Robert F. "Beatrice's 'Pernicious Mistake' in *The Cenci*," *PMLA* 75 (1959): 249-53.

Wilson, Milton. *Shelley's Later Poetry: A Study of His Prophetic Imagination*. New York: Columbia University Press, 1959.

Winstanley, Lilian. "Platonism in Shelley," *Essays and Studies* 4 (1913): 72-100.

Yeats, William Butler. *Ideas of Good and Evil*. London: A. H. Bullen, 1903.

Young, A. B. "Shelley and M. G. Lewis," *MLR* 1 (1906): 322-24.

Index